Rising Light

Rising Light

The Promise of Resurrection of the Body

Michael Hickey

HAMILTON BOOKS
AN IMPRINT OF
ROWMAN & LITTLEFIELD
Lanham • Boulder • New York • London

Published by Hamilton Books
An imprint of The Rowman & Littlefield Publishing Group, Inc.
4501 Forbes Boulevard, Suite 200, Lanham, Maryland 20706
www.rowman.com

86-90 Paul Street, London EC2A 4NE, United Kingdom

British Library Cataloguing in Publication Information Available

Library of Congress Cataloging-in-Publication Data Available

ISBN 9780761874119 (pbk. : alk. paper) | ISBN 9780761874126 (ebook)

My wife Terri, my four children, and seven grandchildren are each a light in my life. This new book is dedicated to my youngest daughter, Maryellen, who when I thought the Holy Spirit had previously prompted me to write every single book that was ever in me, then prompted her to tell me that I should write still one more about the promise of resurrection of the body. Here it is.

"On those dwelling in a land overshadowed by death, light has arisen." Mt. 4:16

Contents

Chapter 1

H.O.P.E.—Horizon Of Promised Expectation

H.O.P.E.

Resurrection has been described as the rising from the dead and the resumption of new life. Jesus was crucified as our savior and then rose from the dead because God loves us. To experience the love of God allows us to believe in God's promise of our own future bodily resurrection and certainly, requires the eyes of faith. The past and present experiences of being loved by God and in turn by others also enables us to have a Horizon Of Promised Expectation. Our hope is oriented to the future. But our own future resurrection will be brought about by the Holy Spirit who lives within us, empowering us to be filled with Holy Spirit hope in the present moment.

Hope in our own resurrection requires us to have the expectation that because God has already shown us the evidence that God loves us- that means he will keep his promises. Hope in our own bodily resurrection as promised by God allows us to place this hope not only in "God above," in some heavenly perfect world, but "God ahead" in this concrete and imperfect world filled with evil, anxiety, despairing, and the earthly finality of death. One could say that until the hope of resurrection becomes a realized experience for us, all we have is hope and all we are for now is "beloved dust."

In many of the Gospel stories we will be looking at in subsequent chapters of this book, we will find a tremendous struggle to maintain hope in the resurrection of Jesus Christ. The stories will reach their apex when Jesus is arrested, crucified, dies, and is buried. At that time many of the disciples would abandon hope and flee to Galilee. For example, in the Emmaus Road story in the Gospel of Luke we find the disciples feeling totally hopeless. Two

1

of them are relating the events of the past few days to another traveler they meet on the Emmaus Road:

> We had hoped that this was the one to redeem Israel, and besides all this, it is now the third day since this took place. (Lk. 24:21)

They would regain their hope shortly thereafter as they recognize the risen Jesus as their travel companion in breaking open the scriptures and in the breaking of the bread (Lk. 24:30–31). Hope as a virtue is usually found in the middle ground between two extremes. Each of these extremes is a vice. The vice of deficiency is despair, which is anticipated failure. When one is despairing, hope is seen as foolish, unrealistic, and a cruel joke. Here we are beyond the reach of any and all hope. The other extreme is the vice of excess which is presumption. If we are so overconfident as to simply anticipate success as a foregone conclusion, we don't require any hope at all. Here, hope is unnecessary as it is assured. At both extremes, however, we are left "hope-less." Hope is one of the three theological virtues, along with faith and love. What this implies is that these three virtues are not simply the result of human effort but are infused in us as human persons by the grace of God. They work together and are also interdependent. Faith gives us the eyes to see what is now unseen. We cannot fully see God's promised plan for us, nor can we fully see the plan he has for the entire historical universe. This plan began with Jesus's resurrection as the first fruits and will be fulfilled at the end of history with the role of Jesus after his resurrection now being that of the Universal Christ. Jesus Christ no longer belongs to any one religion, nation, or people. The Universal Christ is greater than all religious institutions including Christianity itself. We will discuss more about that in subsequent chapters of this book.

Like the virtue of love, both faith and hope are expansive and therefore inclusive. Because we can't exactly know what the future holds, we as loving Christians, should desire our faith and hope in the resurrection to include as many people as possible, for we have been told in 1st Corinthians that:

> In the end there will be three things that will last, faith, hope, and love, and the greatest of these is love. (1 Cor. 13:13)

Although we cannot fully know God's plan, our faith gives us the hope that love is all there will be in the end. Conversely, hope's role is to give us this Horizon Of Promised Expectation and spur us on to greater faith and love. In terms of our own bodily resurrection, the fact remains, however, that our hope can only take us to the limits of our own human horizons. As we get closer to one horizon, another opens up. Beyond all human horizons and reasoned possibilities, we can only trust in God's providence, his divine mercy, and infinite love for us.[1]

WHAT IS RESURRECTION?

Resurrection is the state of one risen from the dead; in particular, the rising of Christ from the dead and/or the rising again to life of all the human dead before a final judgment. It conveys the sense of resurgence or revival as its Latin root is *surgere* which means "to rise." The doctrine of resurrection can occasionally be associated with later Judaism, more particularly beginning with the Pharisees as opposed to the Sadducees. Typically, however, because of belief in Jesus's resurrection from the dead, and the subsequent development of belief in a bodily resurrection through the spreading of the Gospel, it is moreover associated with the Christian religion.

The expectation of the resurrection of the dead is found in a few books of the Old Testament. For example, in the Book of Ezekiel in the vision of the dry bones (Ez. 37:1–14), there is an anticipation that the righteous Israelites will rise from the dead. Also, the Book of Daniel had further developed the hope of resurrection with both the righteous and unrighteous Israelites being raised from the dead. Following the rising from the dead, there would occur a judgment with the righteous participating in an eternal messianic kingdom and the unrighteous being excluded from this kingdom. However, all would rise from the dead to face a final judgment. There are envisioned to be two groups which are distinguished, one that rises to eternal life, the other to reproach and disgrace (See Dn. 7:9–14; 12:1–13). There is more foretelling of a bodily resurrection from the dead in the Old Testament Books of 2nd Maccabees (7:11; 9:14), Isaiah (25:8, 26:19–21, 53:11–12), and Job (19:25–27).

Furthermore, in Greco-Roman religious thought there had originally developed a belief in the immortality of the soul, but not necessarily in the resurrection of the body. Symbolic resurrection or the spirit having some form of rebirth had been found in some of the Hellenistic mystery religions, such as that of the cultic mystery religion which evolved from belief in the Egyptian goddess, Isis. But postmortem corporeal resurrection, i.e., resurrection of the body, had not become widespread historically or had evolved as a system of religious belief.

The bodily Resurrection of Christ is a central doctrine of Christianity. It is based on the belief that Jesus Christ was raised from the dead on the third day after his crucifixion and that through his conquering of sin, death, and the devil, all true believers will subsequently share in his victory. Those many New Testament biblical verses which support this belief in a bodily resurrection will be discussed in later chapters of this book. The Christian celebration of this resurrection event had historically been called "The Festival of the Resurrection" and eventually was called "Easter." It is THE principal feast day within the Christian churches and in many ways has become more central to the faith as a Christian event than the festival of Christmas which celebrates the event of the birth of Jesus into the world.

The earliest recorded observance of an Easter celebration in the early Christian community comes from the 2nd century, although the commemoration of Jesus's resurrection from the dead probably occurred earlier on without it being recorded or considered as a Christian festival. It is believed that the early Christian community appropriated pagan names and holidays for their highest festivals. One view, expounded by St. Bede was that the name "Easter" derived from Eostre, who was the Pagan Anglo-Saxon goddess of spring and fertility. This view coincides with that of associating the origin of celebrating the festival of Christmas on December 25th to replace the existent pagan celebration of the winter solstice.

Finally, the Greek and Latin term *pascha*, is taken from the Hebrew word *pesach*, which means "Passover." In the Old Testament Book of Exodus, Chapters 11 and 12, God commands Moses to tell the Israelites to mark a lamb's blood above their doors in order that the Angel of Death will pass over them. The Hebrew Passover festival which centered on a lamb which was slain eventually became for Christians, the celebration of Easter. In fact, in a message given before a general audience by Pope John Paul II, The Holy Father had said:

> Christ's resurrection was an event consisting essentially in a passage from death to life. It was a unique event which, like the Passover, took place in the context of the paschal feasts during which the descendants of Israel annually recalled the exodus from Egypt. They gave thanks for the freeing of their forefathers from bondage and exalted the power of the Lord God which was clearly manifested in that ancient Passover . . . While the resurrection is an event that is determined according to time and place, it nevertheless transcends and stands above history.[2]

So, Christ's resurrection is in many ways the new Passover; it became the new Pasch, which must be interpreted against the background of the ancient Passover which prefigured and foretold it. Christ becoming for us the "Lamb of God" had been prophesied most explicitly in the suffering servant passages in the Old Testament book of the Prophet Isaiah written almost 700 years before Jesus walked the earth (see Isaiah 52:13 to Isaiah 53:12).

In part, this is why, in Greece Easter is now called "Pascha." In Italy Easter is called "Pasqua." In Spain, it is "Pascuas" and in Portugal, "Pascoa." In France, Easter is called "Paques." In Holland, Easter is called "Pasen," and in Denmark it is called "Paaske." The Hebrew Passover Festival in many ways became for Christians, the Wedding Feast of the Lamb, the Festival of Resurrection, and finally, Easter. With this event we celebrate the victory of Jesus Christ, the Lamb of God, our "Agnus Dei." We find in the Bible in the New Testament Book of Revelation the following verses which affirm that hope-filled promise:[3]

> All the inhabitants of the earth will worship it (the beast), all whose names were not written from the foundation of the world in the book of life, which belongs to the Lamb who was slain. (Rev 13:8)

> They will fight with the Lamb, but the Lamb will conquer them, for he is Lord of lords and King of kings, and those with him are called, chosen, and faithful. (Rev. 14:17)

> Alleluia! The Lord has established his reign, our God, the Almighty. Let us rejoice and be glad and give him glory. For the wedding day of the Lamb has come; his bride has made herself ready. She was allowed to wear a bright, clean linen garment." (The linen represents the righteous deeds of the holy ones.) Then the angel said to me, "Write this: Blessed are those who have been called to the wedding feast of the Lamb." And he said to me, "These words are true; they come from God." (Rev. 19:6–9)[4]

NOTES

1. "Hope," *Get Goodness*, Michael Hickey, (Landover Md, University Press of America, pp. 85–87). Online https://www.amazon.com/Get-Goodness-Virtue-Power -Good/dp/0761854576.

2. General Audience Pope John Paul II, March 1, 1989, http://www.totus2us.co.uk /teaching/jpii-catechesis-on-god-the-son-jesus/the-resurrection-is-a-historical-event -that-transcends-history/.

3. New American Bible, United States Conference of Catholic Bishops, Washington DC, 2022. All subsequent Bible verses used in this book can be referenced in the New American Bible online edition at https://bible.usccb.org/bible?utm_ source=google-adwords&utm_medium=cpc&utm_content=newamericanbible&utm _campaign=NABRE https://www.merriam-webster.com/dictionary/resurrection See also https://www.britannica.com/topic/resurrection-religion.

4. Ibid. Ch. 1 f.3, see also https://www.merriam-webster.com/dictionary/resurrection See also https://www.britannica.com/topic/resurrection-religion.

Chapter 2

The Foundation of Our Christian Faith

The resurrection of Jesus Christ is at the very heart of our Christian faith. Without the resurrection, there simply is no Christianity. Even the apostle Paul tells us this in 1st Corinthians:

> But if Christ is preached as raised from the dead, how can some among you say there is no resurrection of the dead? If there is no resurrection of the dead, then neither has Christ been raised. And if Christ has not been raised, then empty is our preaching; empty, too, your faith. (1 Cor. 15:12–14)[1]

Paul is stating very simply in the above verses that denial of the resurrection (1 Cor. 15:12) means that there is no such thing as (bodily) resurrection. If that is true, then it has not taken place even in the case of Jesus Christ. This would render our Christian faith to be empty, have no centrality, or to be simply "heart-less." For without belief in both the bodily resurrection of Jesus Christ and the hope of our own bodily resurrection, Christianity would have absolutely no foundation whatsoever. It would be merely an organized religion founded by a good and decent Jewish man who did some amazing miracles long ago and ultimately set a good example by his dying on a cross for us. It would be seen as having a virtuous moral code which emphasized loving God and one another. It is the resurrection of Jesus Christ from the dead and his promise of our own bodily resurrection which makes our Christian faith both different from the other world religions and foundationally a little bit pregnant.

In his letter to the Philippians, Paul will also tell us:

> But our citizenship is in heaven, and from it we also await a savior, the Lord Jesus Christ. He will change our lowly body to conform with his glorified body by the power that enables him also to bring all things into subjection to himself. (Phil 3:20–21)[2]

7

Without this foundation, our faith would be worthless. Upon his dying on a cross, Jesus sent the Holy Spirit from the Father. The Holy Spirit always points to Jesus as our spiritual GPS and the true north on the Christian compass. Because the Holy Spirit lives in us now by virtue of our being Baptized in the Holy Spirit, so does the loving and faith-filled promise of our own future resurrection. More about this in a later chapter. Also, in subsequent chapters we will be looking at the evidence for supporting the historicity of the resurrection. It has been said that historians cannot affirm the facticity of the Gospel accounts because the events surrounding the resurrection are often contradictory. Of course they're contradictory, as they are not simply written by individuals who conferred in every instance to get their facts straight. The inconsistencies are apparent and certainly not irresolvable. Furthermore, these inconsistencies don't lie in the details of the resurrection event. They are at the heart of the narrative. Certainly, this doesn't negate the fact that all of the resurrection accounts in the gospels have an equal claim to historical reliability. Even with inconsistencies in the narratives, the heart of the narrative in all four gospels gives us a remarkably harmonious account of the fundamental historical facts. For example, we can be fairly certain that there was an empty tomb and that the risen Jesus appeared to at least some individuals. There are simply too many credible witnesses to say otherwise.

There is no doubt that the resurrection itself was indeed a miracle of God. But we should not confuse the miraculous with the factual evidence available for supporting the history of that event. The resurrection of Jesus is no doubt a miraculous explanation of the evidence, but the evidence itself is not miraculous nor is it based on the supernatural. Both the empty tomb stories and post resurrection appearance stories are evidence which is accessible to any historian. So, I think any argument that would ensue wouldn't be over the historical facts. The questions would most probably revolve around the best explanation of these facts. It is the conclusions which might probably be different. Regarding conclusions reached from historical evidence, we will mostly be discussing historical conclusions drawn from facts concerning the empty tomb stories and post resurrection appearance stories in the New Testament.

That being said, I would like to offer one more conclusion drawn from my own personal experience, as one situated in the historical process here and now. After all, I am, like you the reader, a person situated in history. I believe, that from my own personal experience, there is sufficient historical evidence for me to conclude that Christ indeed is risen from the dead. Consequently, that would preclude Jesus being just another ancient figure from history like Napoleon or George Washington. Historically, there have been many notable people along the way, whose names would be recognizable to us; however, they have died, were buried, and even though we know them as a historical personage and occasionally are aware of even where they were buried, they have remained dead to us.

The key difference is that the resurrected Jesus Christ is alive today in the power and presence of the Holy Spirit and thus can be known through the experience of the Holy Spirit dwelling in myself and countless other believers in the historical process. The Apostle Paul tells us in 1st Corinthians:

> Do you not know that your body is a temple of the Holy Spirit within you, whom you have from God, and that you are not your own? (1 Cor. 6:19)

God in the Holy Spirit sent by Jesus Christ from the Father has become an experiential historical reality for me in my life at this present moment in time in the entire historical process. In the Gospels, John the Baptist prophesies that there is one coming who is "mightier" than he and he is not worthy to "fasten his sandal strap." Furthermore, he will "baptize you in the Holy Spirit (Mk. 1:7–8)." Every day, I celebrate the resurrection of Jesus Christ in knowing that through the Holy Spirit alive in me, as well as others, that Jesus is alive. Every sunrise I experience is a celebration of Jesus's rising and a reminder to me of his glorious victory over sin and death and that he is now alive in the presence and power of the Holy Spirit at the core of our being.

Many Catholic Christians call this being "Baptized in the Holy Spirit." Some Protestant Christians call this being "Born Again." Either way, this is a life transforming experience that has occurred in any Christian who is experiencing the love of Christ poured into our hearts through the Holy Spirit. It manifests itself by producing what is called "The Fruit of the Spirit" in one's life, i.e., "love, joy, peace, patience, kindness, generosity, faithfulness, gentleness, and self-control. (Gal. 5:22)." When the Bible talks about the "Fruit of the Spirit," it is referring to the nine attributes that exhibit themselves and are maturing in the life of any Christian who is filled with the Holy Spirit of God. The "Fruit" is the true measure of the power and presence of the Holy Spirit in the life of any Christian. They are called "Fruit" in the singular and not the plural, i.e., "Fruits," by the Apostle Paul in Galatians 5:22, because they all flow from love—love of God and love of others. Without love, there is no "Fruit," nor can there be joy, peace, patience, kindness, generosity, faithfulness, gentleness, or self-control.

In Catholics, it brings alive the Holy Spirit given to us as believers in the Sacraments of Baptism and Confirmation. Baptism in the Holy Spirit deepens the loving communion one has with the risen Lord as well as with others. It also allows one to see the sacramental presence of God in everyone and everything God has created. This sacramentality transcends the bounds of the ritualistic Sacraments of our faith and is tantamount to often seeing the invisible God of mystery all around us in what we might call visible reality.

In particular, the church and receiving the Sacrament of the Eucharist begins to grow in importance in our lives. It then brings to life a love of Sacred Scripture and subsequent reading of the Bible, as well as an active life of daily prayer. This is manifested in every phase of our daily life as one essentially becomes a "contemplative in action." Baptism in the Holy Spirit is, of course, a gift experienced through the loving grace of God and is not dependent or earned due to any merit on our part. It is basically a "sweet surprise of the Spirit" or "amazing grace."[3]

Therefore, I will simply end this chapter by saying that if you are looking for one of the best explanations of the facts of the resurrection, in addition to the two-thousand-year-old historical evidence, you might want to seek to possibly include yourself in the historical process. Think about picking up the Bible and begin reading the New Testament. What strengthened my personal conclusions began with simply reading the gospel of John and then, as the Scripture became alive for me, by then taking the living Word of God into daily prayer, both personally and in community. That was the beginning of a whole new life where I have experienced not only more love, joy, peace, and other fruit of the Holy Spirit (Gal. 5:22), but also more meaning and purpose in my life than what had previously been there. I now consider myself as being part of the historical evidence for affirming the facticity of the resurrection of Jesus Christ from the dead. He is risen indeed and one of the best proofs of his real presence in history today is the Eucharistic experience of the power and presence of his Holy Spirit that he sent from the Father. This experience of Jesus resurrection is now living within us who are now situated in history, and it is this same Holy Spirit who bears the hope-filled promise of a glorious bodily resurrection which is anchored beyond all our earthly horizons and will be realized throughout eternity.

NOTES

1. Ibid. Ch. 1, f. 3.

2. Ibid. Ch. 1, f. 3.

3. *Baptism in the Holy Spirit Handbook*, published by National Service Committee of CCR (Locust Grove, Va., 2012, pp. 13–60).

Chapter 3

The Early Christian Community and Resurrection History

The earliest first century followers of Jesus (Jewish-Christians) understood him as the Son of Man in the Jewish sense, an angelic-human, obedient to God, resurrected from the dead, in a glorified body, exalted to heaven, and ready to return as the Son of Man (the figure described by Daniel in Chapter 7:13–14). As Messiah, he would usher in the Kingdom of God and rule over it as its King.

Saul, the Jew, after his experience on the Damascus Road had become the Apostle Paul about 35 AD. Thus, the earliest mention of Jesus's resurrection will be recorded in Paul's epistles and not the gospels as many might imagine. Unlike the four canonical gospels which would follow, Paul shows less interest in the teachings of Jesus. Instead, his focus is on Jesus's role as the suffering, crucified, dying, and then risen Christ. However, at the time of his writing (C.-56 AD), he had already moved away from this previously mentioned apocalyptic tradition towards a position where Jesus as Lord and Christ, was no longer the one who proclaimed the message of the coming Kingdom, but instead IS the Kingdom. The Kingdom of God was in Jesus the Christ, and as God's anointed, he became the one in whom the Kingdom of God was and is already present.[1]

This is also the message of the Gospel of Mark, the first canonical gospel written. This gospel is written by a gentile Christian writing for a church of gentile Christians about ten years after Paul, and as early as 60 AD. Although Mark is the shortest of the four canonical gospels, it is the most detailed and vivid. It provides us with a breathless and nonstop narrative as it moves quickly from one story to another. For Mark and his gentile Christian community, Jesus as "Son of God" through his suffering and death by crucifixion and eventual resurrection was essential to God's plan for the salvation and redemption of humanity. Unlike the Apostle Paul, Mark is heavily focused on the teachings of Jesus, his parables, and his miracles.

11

A breakthrough seemingly comes with Peter's confession that Jesus is the Christ (Mk. 8:27–30), but Jesus himself emphasizes his passion (Mk 8:31; 9:31; 10:33–34). Jesus, the "Son of God" is depicted in Mark as moving obediently along the way to his cross in Jerusalem. In Mark, there is considerable emphasis on the Kingdom of God which is an open secret. Because the Kingdom is in Jesus, it shows that God's reign is now breaking into history and humanity. The Gospel of Mark ends in the most ancient manuscripts with an abrupt scene at Jesus's tomb, which the women find empty (Mk. 16:1–8). Here, Jesus's own prophecy, given earlier on in Mk. 14:28 is reiterated, that the risen Jesus will go before the disciples into Galilee; "there you will see him as he told you (Mk. 16:7)." In the ancient manuscripts, these words may have implied that there would be post-resurrection appearances there. In the longer ending (Mk. 16: 9–20) which is believed to have been added by a disciple of Mark just before the beginning of the 2nd century, there are, in fact, some post-resurrection appearances which occur later in the historical process. Some of these mentioned in the longer ending of Mark's gospel are confirmed in Luke's and John's gospels (see Lk. 24 and John 20).[2]

From the onset of his gospel, Matthew will include an infancy narrative that follows the genealogy. Here, the mystery of Jesus's person is declared. He is conceived of a virgin by the power of the Spirit of God (Mt. 1:18–25). This is the first of this gospel's fulfillment citations whose purpose is to show that he was the one to whom the historical prophecies of Israel (see Is. 7:14), were pointing: "He shall be named Emmanuel, for in him God is with us (Mt. 1:23)." At the end of this gospel, Matthew has Jesus claiming: "all authority in heaven and on earth" (Mt. 28:18) and he presents Jesus's appearance in Galilee as the human body, resurrected, transformed, and glorified (Mt. 28:19–20). Matthew will envision the breaking-in of the new and final age through Jesus's ministry, but more particularly through the crucifixion, death, and resurrection of Jesus in history. The passion and hence the resurrection of God's Son means nothing less than the turn of the ages, a new stage of history. Although the old age continues, as it will until Jesus's triumph at his second coming, the final age has now begun. This is known only to those who have seen the Risen One and to those, both Jews and Gentiles, who have believed and have themselves become his disciples (cf. Mt. 28:19). To them he is risen and constantly, though invisibly, present (Mt 28:20). At the beginning and at the end of his gospel, Matthew will verify many of the historical promises recorded in the books of the Old Testament as having been fulfilled in Jesus with the name Emmanuel, "God is with us" (cf. Mt. 1:23). For Matthew, God is always with us at all places and times in the course of history.[3]

Luke will present his gospel mostly from a historical perspective which he shows as having continuity between the history of Israel and the life, death, and resurrection of Jesus Christ. Jesus would fulfill the Old Testament prophecies (Lk. 4:21; 18:31; 22:37; 24:26–27, 44). This would be a two-volume work, Luke/Acts, that continues the biblical history of God's dealings with humanity found in the Old Testament. It would further show how God's promises to Israel have been fulfilled in Jesus and how the salvation promised to Israel and accomplished by Jesus has been extended to the Gentiles.

To accomplish his purposes, Luke will also show that the preaching and teaching of the representatives of the early church are historically grounded in the preaching and teaching of Jesus, who during his ministry (Acts 1:21–22) prepared his specially chosen followers and commissioned them to be witnesses to his promised resurrection and to all else that he did (Acts 10:37–42). This historical continuity between the Old Testament, the ministry of Jesus, the resurrection of Jesus Christ, and the ministry of the apostles is Luke's way of guaranteeing the fidelity of the Church's teaching to the teachings and prophecies of Jesus. Luke will argue in Acts that early Christianity is the logical development and proper fulfillment of historical Judaism. Luke's story of Judaism, Jesus's cross and resurrection, and the Early Christian church is dominated by this continuing historical perspective.[4]

In the synoptic gospels of Mark, Matthew, and Luke, Jesus is portrayed as having the highest status of humanity, but the ancient Jewish commitment to monotheism prevents these three authors from depicting him as fully one with God. This stage is reached first in the Johannine Christian community, as John the Beloved Apostle, writing the last canonical gospel almost toward the end of the first century in 90–95 AD, writes a gospel from an entirely different perspective than the others. The other canonical gospels will end up being termed as "synoptic" because they are parallel, harmonious, and show considerable evidence of borrowing from each other. John's gospel will emphasize an entirely different historical beginning as he begins his gospel with not the human, but the divine origins of Jesus Christ. John will tell us of Jesus's pre-existence and how, as the Logos, he will become for us the summation of all intelligible reality. Here in this New Testament gospel, Jesus becomes God incarnate, and we are told that he has a central role in creation and the ordering of the entire universe. Toward the end of John's gospel, as he views and experiences the resurrection of Jesus's body, and puts his fingers in the nail marks, even doubting Thomas will have to exclaim:

My Lord and my God. (Jn. 20:29)

Jesus's response, as recorded by John, is perhaps not only intended for doubting Thomas and the early Christian church, but for us today who want to know more about the history of Jesus's resurrection:

Jesus said to him, "Have you come to believe because you have seen me? Blessed are those who have not seen and have believed. (Jn. 20:30)[5]

SON OF MAN

If Jesus is now risen and deemed to be the Son of God, then who is this mysterious Son of Man figure? At the end of the first Chapter of John following the Logos Prologue, Jesus will be found among the first disciples who are each asked by another discile in turn to "come and see." John will first use the title "Son of Man" in a revelation by Jesus to Nathanael as one of the first disciples:

And he said to him, "Amen, amen, I say to you, you will see the sky opened and the angels of God ascending and descending on the Son of Man." (Jn. 1:51)

Son of Man was the primary title Jesus used throughout all four Gospels to describe or refer to himself. But what do you think the title "Son of Man" meant to John and to Jesus? Jesus refers to himself eighty times in all four Gospels as "Son of Man," including ten times in John's Gospel.

In a dialogue with Nicodemus, as He did with Nathanael, Jesus will again use the title twice more referring to his ascending and descending from heaven and being born from above. Furthermore, listen closely to John's words in the third chapter of his Gospel as he refers to Jesus as both "Son of Man" and "Son of God." Here is what he says:

"No one has ascended to heaven except the one who has descended from heaven, the Son of Man. And just as Moses lifted up the serpent in the desert, so must the Son of Man be lifted up, so that everyone who believes in him may have eternal life." For God so loved the world that he gave his only Son, so that everyone who believes in him might not perish but might have eternal life. For God did not send his Son into the world to condemn the world, but that the world might be saved through him. Whoever believes in him will not be condemned, but whoever does not believe has already been condemned, because he has not believed in the name of the only Son of God. (Jn. 3:13–18)

This will soon be followed by Jesus's declaring to all who were following him and listening, that as the "Son of Man" he has descended from heaven, being sent on a mission to mankind by the Father. There are several references to the "Son of Man" also being the "Son of God" here as well. Jesus will go as far as to declare that he and God the Father are one. He will declare that, following his resurrection, he will have been given the power to receive honor, to send the Spirit, to offer eternal life to all who believe in him, and to judge humankind.

As God the Father's Ambassador, Jesus has come into the world as its light. There will be several references to the Son of Man being "lifted up." This can be seen on many prophetic levels including Jesus later being glorified while lifted up on the cross, Jesus rising and being lifted up from the dead, and finally, Jesus lifted up from the earth and ascending back to the Father in heaven:

> So must the Son of Man be lifted up . . . So Jesus said (to them), "When you lift up the Son of Man, then you will realize that I AM, and that I do nothing on my own, but I say only what the Father taught me . . . So the crowd answered him, "We have heard from the law that the Messiah remains forever. Then how can you say that the Son of Man must be lifted up? Who is this Son of Man?" (Jn. 3:14; 8:28; 12:34)

Ordinarily, "Son of Man" could be just an oblique way of referring to your own self with special reference to your human fragility and frailty. Just as the title "Son of God" could sometimes refer to Jesus's divinity, "Son of Man" could sometimes refer to Jesus's humanity, but it's not all as simple as that. There is more to it. In the Old Testament, the prophet Ezekiel used the title "Son of Man" more than Jesus did in the Gospels; ninety-four times in fact. There are some similarities to the manner in which Jesus used the title, especially in Matthew, Mark, and Luke. The title in Ezekiel is used more as a common idiom to express that it is a human being and distinct from the divine. However, the use of this title by Jesus in John's Gospel is very different than what is implied by Ezekiel or what it often implies in the synoptic Gospels. Rather than use the "Son of Man" title the way Ezekiel did, John seems to use the title more in line with the reference to it in the Old Testament Book of Daniel. In Daniel, worldly kingdoms are typically represented by grotesque beasts, but the coming of the eternal Kingdom of God is represented by the "Son of Man" who receives dominion, power, worship, and Kingship. In Chapter 7:13–14 Daniel writes:

> As the visions during the night continued, I saw coming with the clouds of heaven One like a "Son of Man." When he reached the Ancient of Days and was presented before him, He received dominion, splendor, and kingship; all nations, peoples and tongues will serve him. His dominion is an everlasting dominion that shall not pass away, his kingship, one that shall not be destroyed. (Dn. 7:13–14)

John will reaffirm this intended usage and implications of the title "Son of Man," not only in his Gospel but in the Book of Revelation which he authored after his Gospel was written (see Rv. 1:13, 14:14). In the Book of Revelation, here is what John writes:

> And in the midst of the lampstands (stood) one like a Son of Man, wearing an ankle-length robe, with a gold sash around his chest. (Rv. 1:13)

And:

> Then I looked and there was a white cloud and sitting on the cloud one who looked like a Son of Man, with a gold crown on his head and a sharp sickle in his hand. (Rv. 14:14)

The title "Son of Man" which Jesus uses to refer to Himself in John's Gospel describes one who is more a kind of human intermediary figure, a God-Man, a transformed human, both who descended from the world above and who, following his resurrection from the dead, is ascending back to the Father in heaven. In John's Gospel, He is the Logos figure who first descends from heaven to become the point of contact between heaven and earth. He brings with Him, heavenly glory, power and authority. Following his rising from the dead, he will have the ability to destroy evil and death, judge men, offer eternal life, send the Holy Spirit from the Father, and establish God's reign on earth. "Son of Man," when used by Jesus to refer to himself in John's Gospel, doesn't just refer to his humanity as we know it, just as being God's Son and the second person of the Trinity is more than being a son of God. For, we are told in Luke's Gospel that even Adam could claim to be a son of God (Lk. 3:38). Just so, when Jesus refers to Himself as "Son of Man," he is saying more than I am a son of humankind. As "Son of Man," John is describing Jesus as the actual communication of divine life (Jn. 6:53) bringing new birth from above, descending to earth and subsequently imparting this new birth to believers through His Holy Spirit when, following his resurrection, he ascends again.

"Son of Man," as the principal title used by Jesus in the Gospel of John, describes his intimate relationship between being Jesus of Nazareth who descended from heaven in human flesh to be born of Mary by the Holy Spirit and the eternal personal relationship with God the Father and the Holy Spirit he had from the beginning. The title also describes the saving- relationship he has with us and all those who believe in him throughout all time on earth. We see an example of this depicted by John as Jesus restores the sight of the man who was born blind and subsequently comes to believe in Jesus as the Son of Man and worships him:

"Do you believe in the Son of Man?" He answered and said, "Who is he, sir, that I may believe in him?" Jesus said to him, "You have seen him and the one speaking with you is he." He said, "I do believe, Lord," and he worshiped him." (Jn. 9:35)

Unlike the synoptic Gospels of Mark, Matthew, and Luke, John will portray Jesus's death on the cross as the continuous beginning of the Son of Man's hour of glorification as well as the Father's glorification in and through Jesus. This will show his future disciples for all time that the cross of Christ and his subsequent resurrection should be seen as one continuous and glorious event:

The hour has come for the Son of Man to be glorified . . . Jesus said, "Now is the Son of Man glorified, and God is glorified in him. If God is glorified in him, God will also glorify him in himself, and he will glorify him at once." (Jn. 12:23; 13:31–32)

The cross of Christ cannot be separated from his bodily resurrection from the dead and neither should the resurrection of Christ be seen as a separate event from his death on the cross. They are one continuous event. Finally, because Jesus is God-Man, the title "Son of Man" should not be seen to hold any more or less significance than the title "Son of God." They both describe one Being.[6]

NOTES

1. Raymond Brown, ed., *Jerome Biblical Commentary*, "Paul," (Englewood Cliffs, NJ, Prentice Hall Pub., 1968, pp. 215–349).
2. Ibid. Ch. 3, f. 1, "Mark," pp. 21–61 see also M. Hickey, *Holy Silence,* "The Messianic Secret" (Lanham, Md., Hamilton Books, 2021, pp. 87–92).
3. Ibid. Ch. 3, f. 1, "Matthew," pp. 62–114.
4. Ibid. Ch. 3, f. 1, "Luke," pp. 115–164.
5. Ibid. Ch. 3, f. 1, "John," pp. 414–466.
6. Ibid. Ch. 3, f. 1, "Son of man, Son of God," Sections 42–45; 61–68, See also Richard McBrien, ed., *Catholicism* (New York, NY, Harper Collins Pub., 1994, pp. 431–433); see also Ibid. Ch. 1, f. 3.

Chapter 4

Is the Resurrection Strictly an Historical Event?

As was stated at the end of the previous chapter, the cross of Christ and his bodily resurrection from the dead should be seen as one continuous and glorious event. Although we will always have been redeemed historically by the cross of Jesus Christ alone, the resurrection remains as the strongest Christian evidence of Jesus's messianic claims. But it should not be seen simply as a "sequel" to the story because the cross and resurrection is moreover the beginning and not yet the end of the story. If I am writing these words and you are reading them, then death and bodily resurrection has happened for Jesus, but not happened for at least one and possibly both of us.

It was really the resurrection and his witness to it which was the impetus for John the Evangelist to write the fourth Gospel which emphasized the divinity of Jesus Christ, his pre-existence, intimate relationship to the Godhead and all of creation, as well as his role in salvation history. In terms of the resurrection, John will tell us that:

> No one has gone up to heaven except the one who has come down from heaven, the Son of Man. (Jn. 3:13)

And

> What if you were to see the Son of Man ascending to where he was before?" (Jn. 6:62)[1]

As risen and exalted Son of God, Christ would now hold Lordship over the entire universe. He has graced us with his Holy Spirit as the down payment as he became the first born of many who will rise from death to the light of life.

A method commonly used today to determine the historicity of an event is what is called: "Inference To the Best Explanation."[2] Historians describe this as an approach where we begin with the evidence available to us and then infer what would, if true, provide the best explanation of that given historical evidence. This is a kind of historical data reasoning and deduction process where one attempts to arrive at hypothetical conclusions by explaining what the historical data infers. You do this by further eliminating other possibilities. You want to pick the explanation which has the greatest degree of explanatory power and the one which has the highest degree of plausibility based on the accepted knowledge implying the hypothesis. In other words, we ought to accept an event as historical if it gives the best explanation for the evidence surrounding it.

For the purposes of this book, in looking at the resurrection of Jesus historically, I will be relying heavily on the use of the New American Bible and refer often to Biblical verses. Many of my evidential proofs will be taken from verses in the Bible and I will be using what Biblical scholars call the Historical-Critical method[3] in the use of these verses and not taking a fundamentalist approach. The Historical-Critical method takes into account the fact that any biblical text was written long ago, in a society, time, and culture very different from our own. It attempts to understand the texts, first of all, in the context of that ancient setting in order to get at the original intended meaning. Therefore, even though I do believe that the Bible is divinely inspired, this approach will not be arguing that as a Christian I am justified by my faith in the resurrection to conclude my understanding of the resurrection as a potentially historical event. Even though I believe that the Bible is divinely inspired, I will treat the Bible simply as another book of ancient literature used to show evidential proofs. Most skeptics who don't believe in either the divine inspiration of the Bible or the historical reality of the resurrection would at least agree that the Bible as an ancient source can still provide us with some historical data.

In employing "The Inference to the Best Explanation" as an historical approach to the evidence available, I think you will agree that when we look at the evidence, the truth of the resurrection of Jesus Christ seems to emerge clearly as the best explanation. There is no other hypothesis that even comes close to accounting for the evidence. Therefore, there is solid historical grounds for the truth that Jesus Christ rose from the dead. There were no witnesses to the actual resurrection of Jesus Christ from the dead as it occurred. Thus, we are left with other valuable pieces of historical evidence that enable us to view the resurrection as an event which took place in what we understand as the historical process. The earliest and most credible literature mentioning Jesus's resurrection is found in the New Testament. Although the New Testament is perceived as a single volume, it often appears as part of the complete Christian Bible and includes the Old Testament. The New Testament is actually a collection of 27 books and letters written by no less than nine authors within the first century of the Christian church. But not all of the New Testament literature mentions Jesus's resurrection. Those books and letters that do are the four Gospels—Mark, Matthew, Luke, and John—The Book of Acts, some of Paul's letters, 1 Peter, and Hebrews. The textual evidence shows decisively that the Gospels which first circulated in an oral tradition were then written and circulated during the lifetime of most of those who witnessed the events surrounding the crucifixion and resurrection. The New Testament would have never survived had the facts put forth by these witnesses been inaccurate. Minimally, these facts would indicate that each of the four Gospels are at least historically reliable sources.

In the New Testament, we can know that the resurrection took place because of its effects. We can view at least two major occurrences through what we might call a Christian lens supported by concrete evidence. Both the empty tomb and post-resurrection appearances are Biblically based stories from history. They were not witnessed by everyone but only by certain individuals in particular places and times. From its earliest beginnings, because of both its witnesses to the empty tomb of Jesus and the appearances of the resurrected Christ, the followers of Jesus Christ were convinced that he had, in fact, been raised from the dead. For Christ, it was not just a return to a dead and subsequently revivified body in ordinary space and time. He did not simply return to the same body he previously had. The evidence for the empty tomb and the post-resurrection appearances will be demonstrated from every New Testament biblical account in chapters 5 and 6, the next two chapters of this book.[4]

The historical evidence of the empty tomb appears very early on in history beginning with the oral and written traditions of the gospel of Mark, the first canonical gospel written. Because it was composed so early and close to the time of the crucifixion and resurrection of Jesus, it is too early to be considered as a "legendary evolution." What shatters the legendary evolution argument further is that we know that the empty tomb was discovered by women and not men. Women in this kind of Patriarchal society would not generally be considered as credible witnesses. If it were, in fact, a legend, the story would have evolved that it was men who discovered the empty tomb. This would make the story more plausible. The probable reason women are cited as finding the empty tomb must be that this is in fact true to what happened. For the gospel authors to have included women in this Patriarchal society, culture, and time period, would have damaged their claim's credibility. To include women would have simply been counterintuitive to the story being a legend.

As far as reasons for the tomb being empty in the first place, it is not likely that the body was stolen. If the Jews or Romans stole Jesus's body this would have defeated their purpose of trying to destroy Christian belief in the empty tomb giving rise to the appearances of a resurrected Jesus Christ. If the disciples stole Jesus's crucified body, then they were mostly all willing to be martyred and die for a lie. Belief in the resurrected Christ and dying for that belief is entirely plausible; knowing it was a lie, being brutally tortured, and subsequently martyred, that is most unlikely. Liars do not make credible martyrs.

As to the post-resurrection appearance stories, we will see in a future chapter of this book that the Apostle Paul's account is the earliest account. One of the strongest pieces of evidence that scholars look for is whether or not an event is early, close to the date of the actual historical event, or contains eyewitness accounts. It is believed that the Apostle Paul wrote his first letter to the Corinthians from Ephesus even before Mark wrote the first of the four canonical gospels (C.60–65 AD). Paul established the Christian community at Corinth about 51 AD on his second missionary journey. The First Letter to the Corinthians is dated around 56 AD.[5] Paul was executed and died in 65 AD. Most of what Paul had to tell us about the resurrection of Jesus, he relates to us as post-resurrection evidence in The First Letter to the Corinthians, Chapter 15:

> For I handed on to you as of first importance what I also received: that Christ died for our sins in accordance with the scriptures; that he was buried; that he was raised on the third day in accordance with the scriptures; that he appeared to Cephas, then to the Twelve. After that, he appeared to more than five hundred brothers at once, most of whom are still living, though some have fallen asleep. After that he appeared to James, then to all the apostles. Last of all, as to one born abnormally, he appeared to me. (1 Cor. 15:3–8)[6]

It is understood that the Apostle Paul received this account from the apostles Peter and James within six years of the crucifixion of Jesus at a meeting between Peter and Paul in Jerusalem. Six years from the resurrection event would be considered very early on. Firstly, the apostle Paul says he has: "handed on," and then: "what I also received." These two phrases are clues that he is about to quote a statement of faith. As mentioned, Paul wrote 1st Corinthians 15 around AD 56, which is just 26 years after the accounts of Jesus's death and resurrection in AD 30. He tells the Corinthians that he is handing on the statement he also received. This means he received it at an earlier time than AD 56. Peter and James are listed among those eyewitnesses who had seen the risen Christ. They are both testifying to their own two eyes being their "on the scene" witness. A little later in this same letter, Paul will tell us in 1st Cor. 15:23, that Jesus was the first to be raised, but our future bodily resurrection will be tied to his.

Furthermore, as historians review documents of historical significance to determine whether or not an event took place, they look for multiple independent sources of attestation to determine an event's historicity with a higher degree of certainty. Several facts of ancient history are verified by only one source, but multiple sources of attestation in agreement with one another can allow historians to consider the event with a greater degree of certainty. In addition to Paul's account in 1st Corinthians, there are the post-resurrection appearances to the disciples confirmed later in all four of the canonical gospels (see Mark 16:14; Matthew 28:16–17; Luke 24:36, 46–48 and John 20:19). Nonetheless, because most dictionaries and encyclopedias begin with a basic definition of the word, *history*, as "the study of past events," a problem arises.[7]

For those who witnessed the effects of the resurrection, their experience cannot be called anything but historical. On the one hand, because the resurrection of Christ took place outside the confines of time and space and occurred on the other side of Jesus's earthly crucifixion and death, the resurrection could also have historical implications for everyone in the universe at every point in space and time, past, present, and future. Thus, the crucifixion, death, and burial of Jesus Christ is no doubt an historical event. On the other hand, the resurrection of Christ, because of its effects on all of history from beginning to end should moreover be viewed not simply as an historical event but as a "transhistorical" event. This consideration will be discussed in subsequent chapters of this book.

At this point, let me state that I am not simply using the Bible to prove the Bible. I am only attempting to objectively look at the oldest ancient testimonies of those witnesses who had been closest to Jesus in all of history. The gospels and the other books of the New Testament are ancient, individual documents, the closest to the time of Jesus of all documents in history. Each of these books has a separate author or authors and stands on its own independent merit.

After looking at the historical evidence, perhaps the only way you could come to the conclusion that the resurrection should not be considered as any kind of a "transhistorical" event, is if your starting point is not the historical evidence such as the reality of the empty tomb and post-resurrection appearances. These were described by those who were witnesses and saw their effects. Rather you begin with your own conclusion which denies any historical evidence and takes into consideration only that because Jesus was crucified, died, and was buried, he therefore could not possibly rise from the dead. That denial and leap to a quick conclusion takes more faith and belief than any other conclusion and negates any and all historical evidence to the contrary.

Finally, no miracle, even someone rising from the dead, might not be enough evidence to convince anyone to believe. We had already been warned by Jesus in the gospels that:

No sign will be given except that of Jonah. (see Lk. 11:29–32)

There is also the gospel account of the parable of the rich man in torment appealing to father Abraham to send someone from the dead to his five brothers so that they might repent and believe. Here we find a foreshadowing in the gospel of the rejection of the call to repentance even after Jesus's resurrection from the dead:

> He said, "Oh no, Father Abraham, but if someone from the dead goes to them, they will repent." Then Abraham said, "If they will not listen to Moses and the prophets, neither will they be persuaded if someone should rise from the dead." (Lk. 16:30–31)[8]

NOTES

1. Ibid. Ch. 1, f. 3.

2. Douven, Igor, "Abduction, Inference to the Best Explanation" *The Stanford Encyclopedia of Philosophy* (Summer 2021 Edition), Edward N. Zalta (ed.), https://plato.stanford.edu/archives/sum2021/entries/abduction/.

3. Ibid. Ch. 3, f. 1, Section 41: 1–74; 70:1–75:171.

4. See chapter 5 (Empty Tomb) and chapter 6 (Post Resurrection Appearances).

5. Ibid. Ch. 3, f. 1.

6. Ibid. Ch. 1, f. 3.

7. Ibid. Ch. 3, f. 1–5. See also https://www.britannica.com/dictionary/history and https://dictionary.cambridge.org/us/dictionary/english/history and https://www.oxfordlearnersdictionaries.com/us/definition/english/history.

8. Ibid. Ch. 1, f. 3. For further information concerning this chapter, See W.L. Craig, *Reasonable Faith*, online version, https://www.reasonablefaith.org/podcasts/defenders-podcast-series-1/s1-the-doctrine-of-christ/the-doctrine-of-christ-part-18 and *Jesus' Resurrection: Fact or Figment*, W.L. Craig with G. Lüdemann, ed. P. Copan and R. Tacelli (Downer's Grove, IL: Inter-Varsity Press, 2000); see also Behan McCullagh, *Justifying Historical Descriptions*, (Cambridge: Cambridge University Press, 1984), p. 19; W.L. Craig, *The Son Rises: The Historical Evidence for the Resurrection of Jesus* (Chicago, IL: Moody Press, 1981).

Chapter 5

The Empty Tomb Stories

RISING LIGHT

The rising light of Jesus Christ burst forth from the tomb in glory with the morning sunrise, shining to all parts of the earth. Illuminated by the Holy Spirit, the Spirit of truth, it will thus give birth to the spreading of the Gospel of God. The Gospel writers wrote in such a way as to invite readers of the Gospel throughout all time to access the grace and power of the Holy Spirit of Jesus Christ living (yes, alive) in the Word of God. In other words, the Gospel does not merely tell us about the life, ministry, and teaching of Jesus, as much as it brings us into living contact with Jesus in the Holy Spirit sent from the Father. Jesus Christ becomes really present to us in the Word of God in a similar way to his real presence in the Eucharist. Therefore, the Gospel of Jesus Christ gives us more than a history of the resurrection, as it conveys to us the grace of the self-communication of God who is a Holy Mystery.

GOSPEL OF MARK

Mark was a disciple of the Apostle Peter, a direct witness to the resurrection of Christ. Mark is believed to have been the first Gospel written and not Matthew as is listed in the canon. In the empty tomb story as it is written by Mark, (Mk. 16:1–8), The purpose of the narrative is to show that the tomb is empty, and thus Jesus has been raised from the dead (Mk. 16:6). Mark tells the disciples, the early Christian community, and us, that Jesus is going before you to Galilee (Mk. 16:7). This is believed to be stated in fulfillment of what Jesus had said prophetically and was recorded previously in Chapter 14: "But after I have been raised up, I shall go before you to Galilee" (Mk. 14:28).

The Gospel of Mark ends with the discovery of the empty tomb by Mary Magdalene, Salome, and Mary the mother of James. It is the women who find the tomb empty, and a young man stationed there announces to them what has happened. They are then told to proclaim the empty tomb news to Peter and the rest of the disciples in order to prepare them for a coming reunion with the resurrected Jesus. Mark's empty tomb story ends at Mk. 16:8 with the women telling no one because they were afraid. This seemingly abrupt termination caused some to believe that the original ending of this gospel may have been lost.

Mark's Empty Tomb Story

The Resurrection of Jesus

> When the sabbath was over, Mary Magdalene, Mary, the mother of James, and Salome bought spices so that they might go and anoint him. Very early when the sun had risen, on the first day of the week, they came to the tomb. They were saying to one another, "Who will roll back the stone for us from the entrance to the tomb?" When they looked up, they saw that the stone had been rolled back; it was very large. On entering the tomb, they saw a young man sitting on the right side, clothed in a white robe, and they were utterly amazed. He said to them, "Do not be amazed! You seek Jesus of Nazareth, the crucified. He has been raised; he is not here. Behold, the place where they laid him. But go and tell his disciples and Peter, 'He is going before you to Galilee; there you will see him, as he told you." Then they went out and fled from the tomb, seized with trembling and bewilderment. They said nothing to anyone, for they were afraid. (Mk. 16:1–8)

GOSPEL OF MATTHEW

Because it is believed that Mark's Gospel was actually the first canonical Gospel to be written and predates Matthew's Gospel, the empty tomb story found in Matthew (Mt. 28:1–8) most probably was based originally on the Markan account discussed previously (Mk. 16: 1–8). The remainder of Matthew's Chapter 28 is mostly peculiar to Matthew. Although they diverge in thought on some of the details surrounding their empty tomb stories, both Mark and Matthew agree here, that the tomb was in fact empty. Matthew records the exact location of Jesus's tomb. He states:

> And Joseph of Arimathea took the body and wrapped it in a clean linen cloth and laid it in his own new tomb. (Mt. 27:59)

Matthew's empty tomb story is also distinctive in the sense that he has constructed an account that interprets the resurrection event as the turning of the ages (Mt. 28:2–4). Unlike Mark, Matthew also ends his empty tomb account by stating that the women, although they were fearful, were overjoyed as they went to announce the good news of viewing the empty tomb to Jesus's other disciples.

In the Gospel of Matthew, an angel appeared to Mary Magdalene at the empty tomb, telling her that Jesus is not there because he has been raised from the dead, and instructing her to tell the other followers to go to Galilee to meet Jesus. Further on in Chapter 28, Matthew will discuss how the Jewish opposition to Jesus is continuing at the time he is writing his gospel in the present moment. The Jews continue to say that the claim concerning the resurrection of Jesus is a deception which has been promulgated by the disciples who stole his body from the tomb and that was the reason why the tomb was empty (see Mt. 28:11–15).

Matthew's Empty Tomb Story

After the sabbath, as the first day of the week was dawning, Mary Magdalene and the other Mary came to see the tomb. And behold, there was a great earthquake; for an angel of the Lord descended from heaven, approached, rolled back the stone, and sat upon it. His appearance was like lightning and his clothing was white as snow. The guards were shaken with fear of him and became like dead men. Then the angel said to the women in reply, "Do not be afraid! I know that you are seeking Jesus the crucified. He is not here, for he has been raised just as he said. Come and see the place where he lay. Then go quickly and tell his disciples, 'He has been raised from the dead, and he is going before you to Galilee; there you will see him.' Behold, I have told you." Then they went away quickly from the tomb, fearful yet overjoyed, and ran to announce this to his disciples. (Mt. 28:1–8)

GOSPEL OF LUKE

In Luke's empty tomb account, we are told at the end of the previous chapter that it is the women who came from Galilee with Jesus who followed behind and previously saw the tomb and the way in which Jesus's body was laid in it (see Lk. 23:54). The women are subsequently identified as Mary Magdalene, Joanna, and Mary the mother of James; and the others who accompanied them (Lk. 24:10). When the women return to the tomb the following morning at daybreak, they find the stone rolled away, Jesus's body gone, and are greeted by two men in dazzling garments. The men are later referred to as "angels." They are puzzled and terrified as the two angels ask the women: "Why do you seek the living one among the dead (Lk. 24:5)?" and then they first advise them that: "He is not here, but he has been raised (Lk. 24:6)." What follows is a reminder to the women of Jesus's prophetic words foretelling these events to them and the other disciples while they still were with him in Galilee:

> "Remember what he said to you while he was still in Galilee, that the Son of Man must be handed over to sinners and be crucified and rise on the third day." And they remembered his words. (Lk. 24:6b–8)

In the Emmaus Road account, which follows later in this chapter, Luke's empty tomb story is recapped for other disciples on the road (Lk. 24:22–24). In Luke/Acts, in Acts of the Apostles, in his speech on Pentecost, Peter will compare the Patriarch David's tomb with David still in it to Jesus's now empty tomb, and he will have the Apostle Paul in his speech discuss the empty tomb account in the synagogue (see Acts 2:29–32 and Acts 13:29–30).

Luke's Empty Tomb Stories

> But at daybreak on the first day of the week they took the spices they had prepared and went to the tomb. They found the stone rolled away from the tomb; but when they entered, they did not find the body of the Lord Jesus. While they were puzzling over this, behold, two men in dazzling garments appeared to them. They were terrified and bowed their faces to the ground. They said to them, "Why do you seek the living one among the dead? He is not here, but he has been raised. Remember what he said to you while he was still in Galilee, that the Son of Man must be handed over to sinners and be crucified and rise on the third day." And they remembered his words. (Lk. 24: 1–8)

The Road to Emmaus

> Some women from our group, however, have astounded us: they were at the tomb early in the morning and did not find his body; they came back and reported that they had indeed seen a vision of angels who announced that he was alive. Then some of those with us went to the tomb and found things just as the women had described, but him they did not see. (Lk. 24:22–24)

Luke/Acts Empty Tomb Stories

Peter's Speech on Pentecost

> My brothers, one can confidently say to you about the patriarch David that he died and was buried, and his tomb is in our midst to this day. But since he was a prophet and knew that God had sworn an oath to him that he would set one of his descendants upon his throne he foresaw and spoke of the resurrection of the Messiah, that neither was he abandoned to the netherworld nor did his flesh see corruption. God raised this Jesus; of this we are all witnesses. (Acts 2:29–32)

Paul in the Synagogue

> And when they had accomplished all that was written about him, they took him down from the tree and placed him in a tomb. But God raised him from the dead. (Acts 13:29–30)

THE GOSPEL OF JOHN

Comparing John's gospel to the three synoptic gospels is never an easy task. John is always different. He always has a different vantage point. The synoptic gospels are called as such because they are parallel gospels. They are harmonious. In many ways they borrowed material from each other. As the last of the four canonical gospels written (as late as 90 AD), John may have been familiar with the other three (at least Mark) but doesn't show too much evidence in most parts of his gospel of borrowing material from the other three synoptic gospels. With this in mind, the empty tomb story in John is an exception. There are more similarities than dissimilarities. The story of the empty tomb is found in the three Mark, Matthew, and Luke traditions; John's version seems to be a fusion of the latter two. For example, in the opening verse of Chapter 20, it is still dark, and according to Mark the sun had risen. Matthew describes it as "dawning," and Luke refers to early dawn. Here in John, what Mary first sees is the stone removed, not the empty tomb. She runs away and is not directed by an angel/man as in the synoptic accounts. What is very distinctive, however, is that there seems to be some special feature about the state of the burial cloths which caused John, the beloved disciple, to believe. Perhaps the details emphasized that the grave had not been robbed as the Jews were continuously declaring at the time, or even possibly and more intriguing that perhaps the burial cloth which covered Jesus's head bore his image (see Jn. 20:6–8). There is no singular or simplistic reason why the state of the burial cloth might have caused John to believe.

John's Empty Tomb Story

> On the first day of the week Mary of Magdala came to the tomb early in the morning, while it was still dark, and saw the stone removed from the tomb. So, she ran and went to Simon Peter and to the other disciple whom Jesus loved, and told them, "They have taken the Lord from the tomb, and we don't know where they put him." So, Peter and the other disciple went out and came to the tomb. They both ran, but the other disciple ran faster than Peter and arrived at the tomb first; he bent down and saw the burial cloths there, but did not go in. When Simon Peter arrived after him, he went into the tomb and saw the burial cloths there, and the cloth that had covered his head, not with the burial cloths but rolled up in a separate place. Then the other disciple also went in, the one who had arrived at the tomb first, and he saw and believed. For they did not yet understand the scripture that he had to rise from the dead. Then the disciples returned home. (Jn. 20:1–10)[1]

EMPTY TOMB CONCLUSIONS

Finally, unlike the apocryphal Gospel of Peter (9:35–11:44),[2] the New Testament including any of the four canonical gospels does not describe the actual resurrection of Jesus as it occurred. Neither is there any known witness who saw it happen visibly or subsequently recorded it as a historical sighted event. However, what was inferred in the earlier discussions should be restated here as a summation. The four gospels diverge in thought on some and even perhaps many of the details surrounding their empty tomb stories. However, Mark, Matthew, Luke, and John all agree here on at least two key and connected points which could be their valid contributions to forming "a historical perspective":

a. That the tomb was in fact empty.
b. That Jesus appeared in a resurrected body to at least some people.

The four canonical gospels end with the hope-filled and joyous promise of an encounter with the risen Lord and not simply an empty tomb. It should be stated here that as Christians, we do not profess our faith in an empty tomb. An empty tomb, in and of itself, could mean nothing more than that the tomb was empty. It could have been empty for many different reasons. Through over two-thousand years, countless Biblical scholars have outlined many reasons why the tomb was empty other than Jesus rose from the dead. The fact that the empty tomb stories have survived as a Christian belief is totally attributable to their connection to the post-resurrection appearances of Jesus which follow the empty tomb stories. Our faith does not rest in an empty tomb, it rests in the resurrection of Christ from the dead and the effect his resurrection had on those who saw his risen and glorified being.

Having seen the risen Christ, the first disciples especially could make more sense out of the empty tomb and the fact that Jesus's body had not simply corrupted in the tomb or was stolen. Therefore, this would make the post-resurrection appearances of Jesus Christ far more important than the empty tomb stories as something that happened in history. Furthermore, the post-resurrection appearance stories, unlike the empty tomb stories, would be events which became far more central to the continuous history of our two-thousand-year-old Christian faith.

The Holy Spirit, alive in the Word of God, has been described by Jesus in the Gospel as "The Spirit of Truth,"[3] and one definition of truth is "correspondence to reality."[4] Taken together, the accounts of the empty tomb and the post-resurrection experiences which followed them point toward the historical reality of the resurrection as being true. The New Testament accounts of both suggest that there is considerable evidence that it would be highly unlikely that belief in the empty tomb and the appearances of the resurrected Christ would simply appear in written form in the Gospel without a clear basis in the memory of the early Christian community. The post-resurrection appearance stories would not exist without there having been an empty tomb. These will be discussed in the following chapter.

NOTES

1. Ibid. Ch. 1, f. 3; see also Ch. 3, f. 1.
2. Gospel of Peter, translated by Raymond Brown, online, https://www.earlychristianwritings.com/text/gospelpeter-brown.html.
3. See Jn. 14:17, 15:26, and 16:13.
4. "truth" *Merriam-Webster Dictionary* online, https://www.merriam-webster.com/dictionary/truth.

Chapter 6

The Post-Resurrection Appearance Stories

EVIDENCE FROM PAUL

The appearance of Jesus to Paul and his conversion on the Damascus Road is said to have occurred in about 35 AD. It convinced him that Jesus was the risen Lord and Christ, who directly commissioned him to be an apostle, particularly to the Gentiles. Paul's first letter to the church of Corinth provides us with greater insight into the life of an early Christian community of the first generation than any other book of the New Testament. It is believed that the Apostle Paul wrote his first letter to the Corinthians from Ephesus even before Mark, the first of the four canonical gospels was written (60–65 AD). Paul established the Christian community at Corinth about 51 AD on his second missionary journey. The First Letter to the Corinthians is probably dated somewhere around 56 AD. Most of what Paul has to tell us about the resurrection of Jesus, he relates to us as post-resurrection spiritual evidence. However, he does tell us some things about the history of Jesus's resurrected bodily appearance to others after he was crucified and died. The basic problem that Paul is addressing is that some of the Corinthians are denying the resurrection of the dead (1 Cor. 15:12). They view it as simply impossible to imagine how any kind of bodily existence could be viable after death. Therefore, one such historical account recorded by Paul takes place in his First Letter to the Corinthians in Chapter 15. He will speak to the resurrection event three ways:

a. The Resurrection of Jesus Christ (15:1–11).
b. The Resurrection of the Dead (15:12–34)
c. The Manner of the Resurrection (15:35–58)

Paul is declaring here that it wasn't just Peter, James, and the rest of the Apostles that were witnesses to the bodily appearance of Jesus after he rose from the dead. There were some five hundred people, and most were still alive at the time Paul is writing this letter. A fewer number had since died after they saw the resurrected Jesus. Following all these, Jesus lastly appeared to Paul. Paul is indicating that many of these people are still alive. You don't have to simply accept his personal word as the complete testimony of Jesus's bodily resurrection. Many of these post- resurrection witnesses are still around at the time Paul is writing. He is implying that, "You could go and ask them for yourself."[1]

Paul's Post-Resurrection Appearance Story

For I handed on to you as of first importance what I also received: that Christ died for our sins in accordance with the scriptures; that he was buried; that he was raised on the third day in accordance with the scriptures; that he appeared to Cephas, then to the Twelve. After that, he appeared to more than five hundred brothers at once, most of whom are still living, though some have fallen asleep. After that he appeared to James, then to all the apostles. Last of all, as to one born abnormally, he appeared to me. (1 Cor. 15:3–8)

GOSPEL OF MARK

Mark wrote his gospel soon after Paul's first letter to the Corinthians in about 60–65 AD. The material in this gospel which begins with Chapter 16, verse 9, has been referred to historically as "The Longer Ending." This so-called longer ending to Mark's gospel (Mk. 16:9–20) with a much briefer conclusion has traditionally been accepted as a canonical part of the gospel of Mark. Early citations of it by some of the Church Fathers indicate that it was composed much later than the rest of the gospel in 60–65 A.D. It was an addition which was probably written just prior to the second century. The Historical-Critical method of Biblical analysis tells us further that the vocabulary and style indicate that the Longer Ending was either written later by a disciple of Mark or more probably by someone other than Mark. Finally, it is also understood to be a general summation of the verses concerning the post-resurrection appearances of the risen Jesus which reflects material found in Luke Chapter 24 and John Chapter 20. These two particular post-resurrection appearance stories in Luke and John will be discussed later in this chapter. In Mark's Longer Ending we find three post-resurrection appearance stories:

a. The Appearance to Mary Magdalene (16:9–11)

b. The Appearance to Two Disciples (16:12–13)
c. The Appearance to the Eleven (16:14–15).[2]

Mark's Post-Resurrection Appearance Stories

The Appearance to Mary Magdalene

> When he had risen, early on the first day of the week, he appeared first to Mary Magdalene, out of whom he had driven seven demons. She went and told his companions who were mourning and weeping. When they heard that he was alive and had been seen by her, they did not believe. (Mk. 16:9–11)

The Appearance to Two Disciples

> After this he appeared in another form to two of them walking along on their way to the country. They returned and told the others; but they did not believe them either. (Mk. 16:12–13)

The Appearance to the Eleven

> But later, as the eleven were at table, he appeared to them and rebuked them for their unbelief and hardness of heart because they had not believed those who saw him after he had been raised. He said to them, "Go into the whole world and proclaim the gospel to every creature." (Mk. 16:14–15)

THE GOSPEL OF MATTHEW

Following the Empty Tomb Story in Matthew's gospel, where Jesus met and appeared to Mary Magdalene and the other Mary after being resurrected (see Mt.28:1–6), an angel will tell these women:

> "Go quickly and tell his disciples, 'He has been raised from the dead, and he is going before you to Galilee; there you will see him.'" (Mt. 28:7)

The women go away quickly from the tomb. Matthew relates that they are fearful yet overjoyed, and they then run to announce this news to his disciples. This resurrection appearance takes place on the road as Jesus meets the disciples on their way and greets them. They approach Jesus, embrace his feet, and do him homage. There is then a second resurrection appearance that takes place in Galilee as Jesus appears again to the disciples and commissions the eleven to go and make disciples of all the nations. They are given instructions to baptize in the name of the Trinitarian God and he assures them that he will never leave them and will be with them until the end of the age (see

Mt. 28:16–20). In Matthew's gospel account there are at least three additions which refer to Jesus's earlier predictions of his coming resurrection appearances (see Mt. 16:21; 17:23; 20:19).[3]

Matthew's Post-Resurrection Appearance Stories

The Resurrection of Jesus

> And behold, Jesus met them on their way and greeted them. They approached, embraced his feet, and did him homage. Then Jesus said to them, "Do not be afraid. Go tell my brothers to go to Galilee, and there they will see me." (Mt. 28:9–10)

The Commissioning of the Disciples

> The eleven disciples went to Galilee, to the mountain to which Jesus had ordered them. When they saw him, they worshipped but they doubted. Then Jesus approached and said to them, "All power in heaven and on earth has been given to me. Go, therefore, and make disciples of all nations, baptizing them in the name of the Father, and of the Son, and of the Holy Spirit, teaching them to observe all that I have commanded you. And behold, I am with you always, until the end of the age." (Mt. 28:16–20)

THE GOSPEL OF LUKE AND ACTS OF THE APOSTLES

The theme of the Galilean witnesses is a major one in the Gospel of Luke and in Acts. It was used by the early Christian community to signify the continuity between the Gospel teachings of Jesus and the teachings of the early Christian church. This would demonstrate to disciples as believers the fidelity of the church's teachings to the words and promises of Jesus concerning resurrection. In Luke, all of the resurrection appearances take place in and around Jerusalem and a consistent feature of the post-resurrection stories is that the risen Jesus was different and initially unrecognizable. In Luke's gospel account, we find two post-resurrection appearance stories which occur first on the road to Emmaus (Lk. 24:13–16; 33–35) and then as an appearance to the disciples in Jerusalem (Lk. 24:36–48). Here it is emphasized that Jesus ate food which is a detail offered by Luke to confirm Jesus's bodily appearance. In Luke's Acts of the Apostles, Jesus appeared to the apostles for forty days and commanded them to stay in Jerusalem (Acts 1:3). There is also one account attributed to the Apostle Paul in the synagogue. The Christian gospel message proclaimed by Paul in the synagogue was initially received very favorably. Later, due to the gathering of a large number of Gentiles from the city, the Jews became so disconcerted that they ultimately became hostile toward the apostles. In this particular account, Paul will conclude by telling us further that those followers whom Jesus appeared to after his resurrection:

These are [now] his witnesses before the people. (Acts 13:29–31)[4]

Luke's Post-Resurrection Appearance Stories

The Appearance on the Road to Emmaus

Now that very day two of them were going to a village seven miles from Jerusalem called Emmaus and they were conversing about all the things that had occurred. And it happened that while they were conversing and debating, Jesus himself drew near and walked with them, but their eyes were prevented from recognizing him. So, they set out at once and returned to Jerusalem where they found gathered together the eleven and those with them who were saying, "The Lord has truly been raised and has appeared to Simon!" Then the two recounted what had taken place on the way and how he was made known to them in the breaking of the bread. (Lk. 24:13–16; 33–35)

The Appearance to the Disciples in Jerusalem

While they were still speaking about this, he stood in their midst and said to them, "Peace be with you." But they were startled and terrified and thought that they were seeing a ghost. Then he said to them, "Why are you troubled? And why do questions arise in your hearts? Look at my hands and my feet, that it is I myself. Touch me and see, because a ghost does not have flesh and bones as you can see I have." And as he said this, he showed them his hands and his feet. While they were still incredulous for joy and were amazed, he asked them, "Have you anything here to eat?" They gave him a piece of baked fish he took it and ate it in front of them. He said to them, "These are my words that I spoke to you while I was still with you, that everything written about me in the law of Moses and in the prophets and psalms must be fulfilled." Then he opened their minds to understand the scriptures. And he said to them, "Thus it is written that the Messiah would suffer and rise from the dead on the third day and that repentance, for the forgiveness of sins, would be preached in his name to all the nations, beginning from Jerusalem. You are witnesses of these things." (Lk. 24:36–48)

Paul in the Synagogue

And when they had accomplished all that was written about him, they took him down from the tree and placed him in a tomb. But God raised him from the dead, and for many days he appeared to those who had come up with him from Galilee to Jerusalem. These are [now] his witnesses before the people. (Acts 13:29–31)

THE GOSPEL OF JOHN

As the last of the four canonical gospels written, John's gospel was probably written about 90 AD, just toward the end of the first century. Unlike the three synoptic gospels of Mark, Matthew, and Luke, most of John's gospel is written from a different perspective. The gospel contains many details about Jesus's nature, life, and mission not found in the synoptic gospels. The prologue at the beginning of this gospel outlines much more concerning the divinity of Jesus Christ, his pre-existence, and role as the incarnate Word of God. John's gospel is therefore considered as "High Christology." There are four major themes and several sub themes which can provide greater insight into John's overall thought processes and perspective. If you would like more detail on the thematic subject matter contained in John's gospel, please see one of my previous books, *Themes from the Gospel of John.*[5]

There are four post-resurrection appearances which are depicted in John's gospel. Three of these are outlined by John in Chapter 20 which has been considered by many to be the "First Epilogue" and the original ending to this gospel. They are (1) the Appearance to Mary of Magdala (20:11–18), (2) the Appearance to the Disciples (20:19–20), and (3) the Appearance to Thomas (20:24–29). The final verses of Chapter 20 are clearly an original conclusion to this gospel and express its purpose (20:30–31). The last post-resurrection appearance in Chapter 21, the Appearance to the Seven Disciples (21:1–14), occurs in the so-called "Second Epilogue" and is considered a later addition to the gospel of John. The Historical-Critical Bible Study method tells us that this chapter was added later by either John himself, a disciple of John, or an early Christian church member. The first possibility (by John himself), for many reasons doesn't seem very likely. Most of the reasons revolve around there being too many inconsistencies which probably occurred due to subsequent editing by another or even a few other individuals. They indicate an original shorter ending to the gospel which more than likely ended with the first epilogue in Chapter 20. On the other hand, the fourth and last canonical gospel cannot be viewed simply through a historical lens as the narrative had been organized and adapted by John to not simply serve history as much as to serve the evangelist's theological purposes.

Prior to this Second Epilogue, John Chapter 20 ends with an epilogue as well, which seems to bring the whole Gospel to a fitting conclusion. At the end of Chapter 20, John writes:

Now Jesus did many other signs in the presence of the disciples, which are not written in this book; but these are written that you may believe that Jesus is the Christ, the Son of God, and that believing you may have life in his name. (Jn. 20:30–31)

Probably the first question we need to ask ourselves is: "Did John the Evangelist intend to write two epilogues?" As was discussed previously, the Catholic Church typically uses the Historical-Critical Method in studying the Bible. It is generally agreed among most Catholic biblical scholars and theologians that this Second Epilogue, called Chapter 21 was not originally part of John's Gospel when he first wrote it. Most Protestant Christian biblical scholars agree as well. Either way it seems it was added after the original Gospel which ended at Chapter 20.

Having a Second Epilogue appears to be anticlimactic to say the least, but the redactor, whoever it was, may have felt that something called an actual epilogue at the end of John's Gospel gave some necessary balance to the prologue at the beginning of the Gospel. Perhaps another scenario might be that the Second Epilogue was added because the disciple in the early church saw some loose ends that needed tying together because of what was going on in history in the Johannine Community near the end of the first century. There may have been some turmoil or tension which existed between rival groups of Christian believers or some unresolved questions in the community regarding the resurrection of Christ. Whatever was surfacing, however, may have tended toward being heretical and needed to be addressed. There are several other peculiarities in Chapter 21 that make it different than how John, the Beloved Disciple, expressed himself at the location and time and in the language in which he wrote the original twenty chapters of this gospel. These differences concern language in particular and stylistic nuances. In any event, Chapter 21 certainly appears anticlimactic.

Furthermore, in Chapter 21, the Second Epilogue, it does not show us the disciples setting out on the mission of evangelization given by Jesus just prior in Chapter 20. Instead, the disciples go fishing. Huh? The disciples know that it is the resurrected Jesus on the shore, but there is something about his appearance that makes them somewhat uncertain and hesitant. The fish and bread which the disciples share with Jesus for breakfast most likely has some Eucharistic significance.

There is an additional important point that the writer of the Second Epilogue may have wanted to make because of the heresies which had arisen in the church shortly after the original Gospel was written. These heresies surrounded both Jesus's humanity as well as his divinity. Chapter 21 illustrates both the divinity and humanity of Jesus in that Jesus had a resurrected body and that Jesus had a body like our own human body which needed food and drink to nourish it. This post-resurrection appearance is certain evidence of his divinity and his bodily resurrection and the fact that he required food and drink is evidence indeed of his humanity. Later, several of the early Christian church councils such as Nicea, Constantinople, Ephesus, and Chalcedon would confirm Jesus's resurrection, both in his full divinity and his full humanity in the years which followed between 325 to 451 AD.

Finally, even though there is considerable evidence verified through the application of the Historical-Critical method that Chapter 21, the Second Epilogue, was probably a later addition, it appears that the tradition was ultimately derived previously from John the Evangelist directly in an oral tradition. The oral tradition could then have been preserved in written form by some disciple other than the original writer of the previous remainder of the Gospel. The chapter was probably added early on, and not too long after the first twenty chapters were composed. There exists historical evidence that the addition of the Second Epilogue (Chapter 21) occurred in written form well before the widespread dissemination of John's Gospel. Furthermore, there is no historical evidence that this Gospel ever circulated without Chapter 21 included. Consequently, the Second Epilogue is part of every one of the earliest manuscripts recorded and is today considered an intricate part of John's entire canonical gospel. At the time John is writing this gospel, times were very different than when Paul's letters and the synoptic gospels were written. The resurrection of Christ was a world-changing historical event and much more of history had swept by. To put this in the context of an old Bob Dylan song: "The Times They Are a-Changin."[6]

John's Post-Resurrection Appearance Stories

The Appearance to Mary of Magdala

> But Mary stayed outside the tomb weeping. And as she wept, she bent over into the tomb and saw two angels in white sitting there, one at the head and one at the feet where the body of Jesus had been. And they said to her, "Woman, why are you weeping?" She said to them, "They have taken my Lord, and I don't know where they laid him." When she had said this, she turned around and saw Jesus there, but did not know it was Jesus. Jesus said to her, "Woman, why are you weeping? Whom are you looking for?" She thought it was the gardener and said to him, "Sir, if you carried him away, tell me where you laid him, and I will take him." Jesus said to her, "Mary!' She turned and said to him in Hebrew, "Rabbouni," which means Teacher. Jesus said to her, "Stop holding on to me, for I have not yet ascended to the Father. But go to my brothers and tell them, I am going to my Father and your Father, to my God and your God." Mary of Magdala went and announced to the disciples, "I have seen the Lord," and what he told her. (Jn. 20:11–18)

Appearance to the Disciples

> On the evening of that first day of the week, when the doors were locked, where the disciples were, for fear of the Jews, Jesus came and stood in their

midst and said to them, "Peace be with you." When he had said this, he showed them his hands and his side. The disciples rejoiced when they saw the Lord. (Jn. 20:19–20)

Appearance to Thomas

Thomas, called Didymus, one of the Twelve, was not with them when Jesus came. So, the other disciples said to him, "We have seen the Lord." But he said to them, "Unless I see the mark of the nails in his hands and put my finger into the nail marks and put my hand into his side, I will not believe." Now a week later his disciples were again inside and Thomas was with them. Jesus came, although the doors were locked, and stood in their midst and said, "Peace be with you." Then he said to Thomas, "Put your finger here and see my hands, and bring your hand and put it into my side, and do not be unbelieving, but believe." Thomas answered and said to him, "My Lord and my God!" Jesus said to him, "Have you come to believe because you have seen me? Blessed are those who have not seen and have believed." (Jn. 20:24–29)

The Second Epilogue: The Resurrection Appearance in Galilee

The Appearance to the Seven Disciples

After this, Jesus revealed himself again to his disciples at the Sea of Tiberias. He revealed himself in this way. Together were Simon Peter, Thomas called Didymus, Nathanael from Cana in Galilee, Zebedee's sons, and two others of his disciples. Simon Peter said to them, "I am going fishing." They said to him, "We also will come with you." So, they went out and got into the boat, but that night they caught nothing. When it was already dawn, Jesus was standing on the shore; but the disciples did not realize that it was Jesus. Jesus said to them, "Children, have you caught anything to eat?" They answered him, "No." So, he said to them, "Cast the net over the right side of the boat and you will find something." So, they cast it, and were not able to pull it in because of the number of fish. So the disciple whom Jesus loved said to Peter, "It is the Lord." When Simon Peter heard that it was the Lord, he tucked in his garment, for he was lightly clad, and jumped into the sea. The other disciples came in the boat, for they were not far from shore, only about a hundred yards, dragging the net with the fish. When they climbed out on shore, they saw a charcoal fire with fish on it and bread. Jesus said to them, "Bring some of the fish you just caught." So, Simon Peter went over and dragged the net ashore full of one hundred fifty-three large fish. Even though there were so many, the net was not torn. Jesus said to them, "Come, have breakfast." And none of the disciples dared to ask him, "Who are you?" because they realized it was the Lord. Jesus came over and took the bread and gave it to them, and in like manner the fish. This was now the third time Jesus was revealed to his disciples after being raised from the dead. (Jn. 21:1–14)[7]

NOTES

1. Ibid. Ch. 3, f. 1.
2. Ibid. Ch. 3, f. 2.
3. Ibid. Ch. 3, f. 3.
4. Ibid. Ch. 3, f. 4.
5. Ibid. Ch. 3, f. 5; See also *Themes from the Gospel of John*, Hickey, M. (Lanham, Md., Hamilton Books, 2021, pp. 1–59.
6. Ibid. Ch. 3, f. 5; also Bob Dylan, *The Times They Are A-Changin,* Online, https://www.youtube.com/watch?v=90WD_ats6eE.
7. Ibid. Ch. 1, f. 3, Ch. 3 f. 5; see also Ch. 6 f. 5.

Chapter 7

The Ascension

The Ascension of Jesus Christ can be described as the exaltation of the risen Christ entering into his final glory at the right hand of the Father. This had been foretold in the prophetic Book of Daniel as Daniel's prophecy spoke of a mysterious savior called "one like a son of man" ascending on a cloud. This mysterious and angelic being approaches the throne of God, where he receives divine glory, honor, and eternal kingship as Daniel writes:

> As the visions during the night continued, I saw coming with the clouds of heaven One like a son of man. When he reached the Ancient of Days and was presented before him, He received dominion, splendor, and kingship; all nations, peoples and tongues will serve him. His dominion is an everlasting dominion that shall not pass away, his kingship, one that shall not be destroyed. (Dn. 7:13–14)[1]

At its center, the Ascension signifies a transition of the risen Christ to that of the Exalted Christ. It is certainly linked with his resurrection, but also with his continuing Eucharistic and Holy Spirit presence in the church as the Body of Christ, his Paschal Mystery, his glorification, and his Second Coming (Parousia). In Christ's human nature, the humanity in which we all have a share, has entered into the inner life of God in a new and exalted way. What this implies is that "heaven" now means that the human person has a place in the heart of God. This exaltation and ascension is hidden from the eyes of much of the world. It is a veiling which is indicated in Scripture throughout the Old Testament and in the New Testament through the continual reference to a "cloud" (Ex. 24:15; Acts 1:9).

The Gospels, as well as The Book of Acts tell us that Christ's Ascension occurred forty days after his Resurrection. Here is what appears in The Gospels of Mark and Luke and the Book of Acts:

> And so, the Lord Jesus, when he had finished speaking to them, was taken up to heaven, and is seated now at the right hand of God. (Mk. 16:19)

Also:

> When he had led them out as far as Bethany, he lifted up his hands and blessed them; and even as he blessed them, he parted from them, and was carried up into heaven. (Lk. 24:50–51)

And:

The Ascension of Jesus.

> When they had gathered together they asked him, "Lord, are you at this time going to restore the kingdom to Israel?" He answered them, "It is not for you to know the times or seasons that the Father has established by his own authority. But you will receive power when the Holy Spirit comes upon you, and you will be my witnesses in Jerusalem, throughout Judea and Samaria, and to the ends of the earth." When he had said this, as they were looking on, he was lifted up, and a cloud took him from their sight. While they were looking intently at the sky as he was going, suddenly two men dressed in white garments stood beside them. They said, "Men of Galilee, why are you standing there looking at the sky? This Jesus who has been taken up from you into heaven will return in the same way as you have seen him going into heaven." (Acts 1:6–11)

The Ascension of Christ is similarly discussed in Lk. 24:51; Eph. 4:8–10; and 1 Pt. 3:22. Also, In the Gospel of John, Jesus will prophecy as follows:

> And I, when I am lifted up from the earth, will draw all men to myself. (Jn. 12:32)

Initially, this would signify Jesus being "lifted up" on the cross. Ultimately, it would announce his Ascension into heaven. Being "lifted up" in the Ascension will mark his exaltation and the definitive entrance of his human-ity into God's heavenly domain where he is seated at the right hand of God to intercede on our behalf. Furthermore, in four other chapters in the Gospel of John, Jesus had already prophesied that his Ascension was to occur after his resurrection (see Jn. 1:51; 3:3, 7, 13, 31; 6:61–62; 20:17). And the factuality of its occurrence was later discussed among his followers in the Apostle Paul's Letters to the Ephesians (4:8–10) and 1 Timothy (3:16). In the Resurrection and Ascension, Jesus of Nazareth would rise and ascend to become the Universal Christ, having been given supreme authority from the Father and exalted Lordship over all of creation. Several centuries after John's Gospel was written, these Johannine verses above would be used in part to not only make reference to the Ascension of Jesus Christ, but also to form a statement of Christian creedal belief. They would help to form what we now refer to as "The Apostle's Creed" in which we recite:

He ascended into heaven and is seated at the right hand of God, the Father Almighty.[2]

Jesus himself had told his disciples that he was going to go away, because only then would he send them the Holy Spirit from the Father (Jn. 16:7–16). And that is what happened on the Day of Pentecost, ten days after Jesus's Ascension. The Holy Spirit descended on the church with awesome power, thus inaugurating a new age in the history of the world- the age of the Holy Spirit. The Apostle Peter connects Jesus's Resurrection, Exaltation, and Ascension with the outpouring of the Holy Spirit on the people of God as follows:

God raised this Jesus; of this we are all witnesses. Exalted at the right hand of God, he received the promise of the Holy Spirit from the Father and poured it forth, as you see and hear. (Acts 2:32–33)

The Ascension was not simply the last of Jesus's resurrection appearances; it is different. Jesus suddenly disappears while the apostles watch. After the resurrection, Jesus appears as different, but in recognizable form. Here Jesus will say to Mary Magdalene, "Stop holding on to me, for I have not yet ascended to the Father (See Jn. 20:11–18, 21:1–14)." However, after his Ascension he will be transformed. His appearance on the Emmaus Road (Lk. 24:13–35) and Saul's experience of Jesus appearing to him on the Damascus Road are evidence of this (Acts 9:1–19). The conversion of Paul under the influence of his experience of Jesus transformation will be even further proof as Paul will become a divinely chosen instrument in the plan of God.

St Augustine, an early church Father, theologian, and often referred to as "The Doctor of Grace," said this about the Ascension and our own future bodily resurrection in one of his homilies given on the Feast of the Ascension:

Today our Lord Jesus Christ ascended into heaven; let our hearts ascend with him. Listen to the words of the Apostle: If you have risen with Christ, set your hearts on the things that are above where Christ is seated at the right hand of God; seek the things that are above, not the things that are on earth. For just as he remained with us even after his ascension, so we too, are already in heaven with him, even though what is promised us has not yet been fulfilled in our bodies.[3]

And in the Middle Ages, St Thomas Aquinas in his *Summa Theologica* describes the necessity for the Ascension to have followed Christ's Resurrection with these words:

The place ought to be in keeping with what is contained therein. Now by His Resurrection Christ entered upon an immortal and incorruptible life. But whereas our dwelling-place is one of generation and corruption, the heavenly place is one of incorruption. And consequently, it was not fitting that Christ should remain upon earth after the Resurrection; but it was fitting that He should ascend to heaven.[4]

The Ascension of Jesus will prove to be not only a disappearance, but also a parting which will end only at the Second Coming of Christ at the Parousia. On the other hand, Jesus had already told us that he will be with us always, until the end of time. So, his ascended presence should be seen more as a transformation than a total absence. Anytime and anyplace where the Holy Spirit in us as believers meets the real presence of Christ in the Eucharist there is continuing evidence of this. Furthermore, this is also an indication that in the here and now, the so-called "present," we can enter into both Christ's present and our own future bodily resurrection, transformation, and ascension.

Because of the mysterious nature of the Ascension, there may be a tendency on the part of some scholars and theologians to overly spiritualize it. If the resurrection is a bodily occurrence and we are to believe in a future Resurrection of the Body, how could we believe that the Ascension of Jesus is strictly something spiritual and not corporeal? Aquinas argued against this in his *Summa* as follows:

The more exalted place is due to the nobler subject, whether it be a place according to bodily contact, as regards bodies, or whether it be by way of spiritual contact, as regards spiritual substances; thus a heavenly place which is the highest of places is becomingly due to spiritual substances, since they are highest in the order of substances. But although Christ's body is beneath spiritual substances, if we weigh the conditions of its corporeal nature, nevertheless it surpasses all spiritual substances in dignity, when we call to mind its dignity of union whereby it is united personally with God. Consequently, owing to this very fittingness, a higher place is due to it above every spiritual creature. Hence Gregory says in a Homily on the Ascension (xxix in Evang.) that: "He who had made all things, was by His own power raised up above all things' . . . This comparison may be considered either on the part of the places; and thus there is no place so high as to exceed the dignity of a spiritual substance: in this sense the objection runs. Or it may be considered on the part of the dignity of the things to which a place is attributed: and in this way it is due to the body of Christ to be above spiritual creatures."[5]

Furthermore, in his book, *Miracles,* the Christian writer and apologist C. S. Lewis for another, objects to any strict spiritualization of the Ascension of

Jesus Christ. He insists that after the Ascension, Christ was not exclusively a spiritual being. Here is what he writes:

> We can (spiritualize the Ascension) only if we regard the Resurrection appearances as those of a ghost or hallucination. For a phantom can just fade away; but an objective entity must go somewhere—something must happen to it. And if the Risen Body were not objective, then all of us, whether Christian or not, must invent some explanation for the disappearance of the corpse.[6]

Finally, to many of us as Christian faithful, the Ascension of Jesus Christ, following his resurrection, may seem like it is a kind of separation from us in that Christ has now left us and ascended back to the Father in heaven. But the words of Karl Rahner, one of the foremost theologians of our time, can shed some light on this and bring us some comfort and consolation in this regard. Here is what he writes in one of his books, *The Eternal Year,* regarding the Ascension as it follows the bodily resurrection of Jesus Christ:

> In the incarnation the eternal Word of the Father compressed himself into our flesh . . . my faith and my consolation are centered on this, that in his Ascension, Jesus has taken with him everything that is ours. He has ascended and sits at the right hand of the Father . . . The absolute Logos shall look at me in eternity with the face of a man . . . The Ascension seems to be a separation. But it is separation only for Our paltry consciousness. We must will ourselves to believe in his nearness —in the Holy Spirit.[7]

In conclusion, Jesus Christ, in ascending, has become for us the Kingdom of Heaven. The Ascension of Jesus following his bodily resurrection is a great mystery for us and a profound paradox. Christ ascending and returning to the Father's side ended his post-resurrection appearances which we read about in the previous chapter. On the one hand, this creates in us a source of great sorrow, for he is now absent from us. On the other hand, it is simultaneously a cause of great joy because he has never been closer and more present to us. This comes about through his Holy Spirit which he sent from the Father and is now alive in us as the body of Christ, as well as his presence in his Living Word in the Sacred Scriptures, and in his Real Presence in our celebration of the Eucharist.[8]

NOTES

1. Ibid. Ch. 1, f. 3.

2. Reference Hickey, M. *Themes from the Gospel of John* (Landover, Md., Hamilton Books, 2021, p 97) see also "Apostles Creed" *The Catholic Encyclopedia* online, New Advent, https://www.newadvent.org/cathen/01629a.htm.

3. Augustine, *Sermo de Ascensione Domini*, Mai 98, 1–7: PLS 2, 429–495.

4. T. Aquinas, *Summa Theologica*, Part 3, Q. 57, Art I. See online http://www.newadvent.org/cathen/01767a.htm see also https://www.newadvent.org/summa/4057.htm.

5. Gregory, *Homily on the Ascension* (xxix in Evang.) T. Aquinas, *Summa Theologica*, Part 3, Q. 57, Art I). See online http://www.newadvent.org/cathen/01767a.htm see also https://www.newadvent.org/summa/4057.htm.

6. Lewis, C. S., *Miracles*: A Preliminary Study (New York, NY; Harper One, 2001, pp. 245–267).

7. K. Rahner, *The Eternal Year* (Abingdon, Oxfordshire, UK, Helicon Pub., Ch. 11, 1964), pp. 97–104.

8. https://media.ascensionpress.com/2020/05/21/jesus-ascension-and-the-theology-of-the-body/ See also https://www.newadvent.org/cathen/01767a.htm. Wynne, J. (1907). Ascension. In *The Catholic Encyclopedia*. New York, NY: Robert Appleton Company. Retrieved December 1, 2022 from New Advent: See also Catholic Catechism, CC# 659 to #667, http://www.scborromeo.org/ccc/p1s2c2a6.htm.

Chapter 8

The Assumption

The Assumption refers to the departure of the Blessed Virgin Mary from this life and the assumption of her resurrected body and soul into heaven. Knowledge of this mystery has come down to us through our Apostolic Tradition as there is nothing in the Bible that refers to this event directly. On occasion, various biblical texts are referenced to indirectly demonstrate the appropriateness of the doctrine. For example, Enoch being "taken up" in Genesis 5:4, the prophet Elijah being "taken up" in 2 Kings 2:11, and the Ascension of Jesus into heaven in Luke 24:51, John 6:62; 20:17, and The Book of Acts Ch. 1. In some ways, although, we will not be "assumed" into heaven, The Assumption of Mary can be seen as a pledge of our own future bodily resurrection. In fact, The Catholic Catechism tells us this:

"The Immaculate Virgin, preserved free from all stain of original sin, when the course of her earthly life was finished, was taken up body and soul into heavenly glory, and exalted by the Lord as Queen over all things, so that she might be the more fully conformed to her Son, the Lord of lords and conqueror of sin and death." The Assumption of the Blessed Virgin is a singular participation in her Son's Resurrection and an anticipation of the resurrection of other Christians. (CC#966)[1]

The Assumption is said to have occurred within fifteen years of Christ's Ascension and the location is believed to have been either Jerusalem or Ephesus. The belief in the corporeal resurrection and assumption of Mary is founded on the apocryphal treatise *De Obitu S. Dominae,* (On the Death of Our Lady) by an anonymous writer, but bearing the name of St. John, which is traced to the fourth or fifth century AD. In the genuine writings of the East, it is mentioned in the sermons of St. Andrew of Crete, St. John Damascene, St. Modestus of Jerusalem, and others. In the West, St. Gregory of Tours, (*De Gloria Martyrs/* On the Glory of the Martyrs, I, no.4) mentions it first. Today the belief is deemed universal in both the East and the West.[2]

St. John of Damascus, a Doctor of the Eastern Orthodox Church, is occasionally referred to as "The Doctor of the Assumption" because of his writings. In these writings he calls Mary, "ruler, and our lady," and also "the Queen of every creature." According to St. John of Damascus, it was St. Juvenal, Bishop of Jerusalem, at the Council of Chalcedon in the year 451, who made known to the Emperor, Marcian, who wished to recover the body of the Mother of God, that Mary died in the presence of all the Apostles. On the other hand, her tomb when opened, upon the request of St. Thomas, was found empty. The apostles at that time concluded that the body was taken up to heaven.[3]

It wasn't until the year 1950 that Pope Pius XII in his Apostolic Constitution, *MUNIFICENTISSIMUS DEUS* (On the Bountiful God) declared infallibly that the Assumption of the Blessed Virgin Mary was a dogma of the Catholic Faith. Pope Pius was not declaring the church's belief in the Assumption as something altogether new in 1950 as there was written evidence of the belief as early as the 4th century. However, here is what this particularly recent Vatican Document relates:

God, who from all eternity regards Mary with a most favorable and unique affection, has 'when the fullness of time came' put the plan of his providence into effect in such a way that all the privileges and prerogatives he had granted to her in his sovereign generosity were to shine forth in her in a kind of perfect harmony. And, although the Church has always recognized this supreme generosity and the perfect harmony of graces and has daily studied them more and more throughout the course of the centuries, still it is in our own age that the privilege of the bodily Assumption into heaven of Mary, the Virgin Mother of God, has certainly shone forth more clearly . . . That privilege has shone forth in new radiance since our predecessor of immortal memory, Pius IX, solemnly proclaimed the dogma of the loving Mother of God's Immaculate Conception. These two privileges are most closely bound to one another . . . Now God has willed that the Blessed Virgin Mary should be exempted from this general rule. She, by an entirely unique privilege, completely overcame sin by her Immaculate Conception, and as a result she was not subject to the law of remaining in the corruption of the grave, and she did not have to wait until the end of time for the redemption of her body . . . Thus, when it was solemnly proclaimed that Mary, the Virgin Mother of God, was from the very beginning free from the taint of original sin, the minds of the faithful were filled with a stronger hope that the day might soon come when the dogma of the Virgin Mary's bodily Assumption into heaven would also be defined by the Church's supreme teaching authority.[4]

KARL RAHNER'S THEOLOGY ON THE ASSUMPTION

Jesuit theologian, Karl Rahner, in 1951, completed a theological study on "The Interpretation of the Dogma of the Assumption" which was titled *Assumptio Beatae Mariae Virginis* that defended the Assumption of Mary into Heaven. This work had been compiled one year after the Papal Encyclical, defining the dogma, quoted above, was released by the Vatican in 1950. In this study, Rahner put forth the belief that Mary, the Mother of Jesus, did not experience a physical death, but instead was resurrected and assumed bodily into heaven similarly to the Ascension of Jesus, and in accordance with it. Rahner had argued that the "new dogma" defined by Pope Pius XII in 1950 was not in fact new but is present in the writings of the earliest church Fathers. Rahner additionally argued that the special grace that Mary experienced in the form of the Immaculate Conception also extended to the Assumption of Mary and an immediate resurrection of her body while she was still alive. "Among the redeemed," said Rahner, "she was the first." He maintained that Mary's fate at the end of her life in the Assumption anticipated the bodily resurrection of the dead at the end of time. At her Assumption into heaven, she experienced a perfection or completion that other Christians hope for at the second coming of Christ and the resurrection of the dead.

In his writing he had held an opinion that if we understand Mary, then we understand something of ourselves. Rahner wrote, "May the blessed Virgin whose first beginning was holy and pure, pray for us, that we too may become what we are." Rahner stated further that, "We shall see that Mary's fate at the end of her life anticipated the resurrection of the dead at the end of time." At Mary's death, she was assumed body and soul into heaven. It happened immediately, but with the death of other Christians, time passes between the moment of death and the bodily perfection of the final resurrection. The Assumption of Mary's body and soul into heaven illustrates the Church's faith in a providential God who saves us through Jesus Christ. Mary's Assumption anticipates the new creation that will reach its fulfilment at the end of time. As a summation, the Marian dogma put forth in 1950 by the Vatican was viewed by Rahner not to be about Mary alone, but also our Christian hope for bodily resurrection.

Rahner's Jesuit superiors censored the work as being "incomplete" when it was first finished in 1951, and it was not actually published until more than fifty years later in 2004, and some twenty years after Karl Rahner's death. He never lived to see it published. Although he was initially prevented from publishing his theology on the Assumption, the way he had expressed himself in his thesis was hardly revolutionary. In fact, in 1992, forty-one years after the definition of the Assumption, the Catechism of the Catholic Church itself linked Mary's destiny to the Christian hope for resurrection of the body at the end of time. It had stated that:

> The Assumption of the Blessed Virgin is a singular participation in her Son's Resurrection and an anticipation of the resurrection of other Christians. (CCC 1992, no. 966)[5]

Today, in light of the words of the Catholic Catechism, Rahner's words at that earlier point in time seem hardly objectionable today.[6]

CONCLUSION

If bodily corruption is the result of sin, it could be that Our Lady was immediately taken to heavenly glory at the end of her life without experiencing death. Since death and the corruption of the human body are the direct consequences of sin, it was not right that the Virgin Mary who, in the Immaculate Conception, was born free from sin, should be affected by this natural law. However, there is ongoing theological debate even today on whether or not the Mother of our Lord actually died prior to her body and soul being assumed into heaven. In establishing the Dogma in 1950, even Pope Pius XII was very careful and extremely cautious in his wording in stating only that:

> The Immaculate Mother of God, the ever-Virgin Mary, having completed the course of her earthly life, was assumed body and soul into heavenly glory. (section 44)

"Completing the course of her earthly life," does not state that she died. Whether Mary died or not, she would not have been subject to the law of death and the corruption of the grave. On the other hand, it seems more certain that, either way, her time on the earth had come to an end and because of her sinless nature, the Lord would not have allowed her body to undergo any form of corruption.

As was mentioned earlier in this chapter, the earliest known Patristic witness to the belief in the Assumption in the West appears to have been St. Gregory of Tours (d. 593). Here are his words:

> When finally, the Blessed Virgin had fulfilled the course of this life, and was now to be called out of this world, all the Apostles were gathered together from each region to her house . . . and behold the Lord Jesus came with His angels and, receiving her soul, entrusted it to the Archangel Michael and departed. At the break of day, the Apostles lifted the body with the couch and laid it in the sepulcher, and they guarded it awaiting the coming of the Lord. And behold the

Lord again stood by them and commanded that the holy body be taken up and borne on a cloud into Paradise, where now, reunited with (her) soul and rejoicing with the elect, it enjoys the good things of eternity which shall never come to an end.[7]

In addition to being the first mention of the Assumption in the West, what is also somewhat significant here in St. Gregory's words, is the subtle mention of the involvement of the Archangel Michael prior to Mary's glorious Assumption, body and soul into Paradise. This brings to mind references contained in the two last Books of the New Testament of the Bible, The Letter of Jude and the Book of Revelation as follows:

The Letter of Jude, Ch. 1

Similarly, these dreamers nevertheless also defile the flesh, scorn lordship, and revile glorious beings. Yet the archangel Michael, when he argued with the devil in a dispute over the body of Moses, did not venture to pronounce a reviling judgment upon him but said, "May the Lord rebuke you!" (Jude 1:8–9)

This letter of Jude is addressing heretics in the early Christian church who "defile the flesh" and "revile glorious beings." In Jude, verse 9, the writer is quoting from an apocryphal Jewish work, the *Assumption of Moses*.[8] He will soon quote from another apocryphal work, *the Book of Enoch*,[9] in Jude verses 14–15. This might cause one to ask the question, "If the Lord would use the archangel Michael to not allow the devil to have the corruptible body of Moses, principally due to its materiality, would he surely not allow the same for the incorruptible body of Mary through the Assumption of the Holy Mother of God body and soul?

Book of Revelation, Ch. 12

The Woman and the Dragon

A great sign appeared in the sky, a woman clothed with the sun, with the moon under her feet, and on her head a crown of twelve stars. She was with child and wailed aloud in pain as she labored to give birth. Then another sign appeared in the sky; it was a huge red dragon, with seven heads and ten horns, and on its heads were seven diadems. Its tail swept away a third of the stars in the sky and hurled them down to the earth. Then the dragon stood before the woman about to give birth, to devour her child when she gave birth. She gave birth to a son, a male child, destined to rule all the nations with an iron rod. Her child was caught up to God and his throne. The woman herself fled into the desert where she had a place prepared by God, that there she might be taken care of for twelve hundred and sixty days. Then war broke out in heaven; Michael and his angels battled against the dragon. The dragon and its angels fought back, but they did not prevail and there was no longer any place for them in heaven. The huge dragon, the ancient serpent, who is called the Devil and Satan, who deceived the whole world, was thrown down to earth, and its angels were thrown down with it. (Rev. 12:1–9)[10]

This passage can speak to us prophetically on many levels. The child is "caught up" to heaven where he reigns with God. This is reminiscent of the Ascension of Christ. The prepared place of refuge for the woman in the desert is reminiscent of the Assumption. John will also speak about Mary from two viewpoints. The Mother of God is an icon of the church on earth. Just as there is a dwelling place prepared for her beyond the reach of the Devil and Satan (the Accuser), so also there will be a dwelling place prepared one day for the church as the people of God and the body of Christ ("those who keep God's commandments and bear witness to Jesus (Rev. 12:17)." The Messiah's exaltation (The Ascension), the woman's prepared place of refuge (The Assumption), and the future dwelling place prepared for God's people (The Resurrection of the Body), can all be linked with God's victory through the Archangel Michael, the protector of God's people. However, this victory is only made possible because of the enthronement of the lamb of God, our Agnus Dei.[11]

NOTES

1. Vatican Archives, *Catholic Catechism* #966, see online https://www .catholiccrossreference.online/catechism/#!/search/s1.2.3.9.6.

2. See S. Andreas Cretensis, Homilia II in *Dormitionem Ssmae Deiparae*: Pg XCVII, 1079 B.).

3. De laudibus Mariae (inter opera Venantii Fortunati): PL LXXXVIII, 282 B et 283 A. See also https://www.vatican.va/content/pius-xii/en/encyclicals/documents/hf _p-xii_enc_11101954_ad-caeli-reginam.html).

4. Apostolic Constitution, *MUNIFICENTISSIMUS DEUS* (On the Bountiful God, Sections 3–6, Pope Pius IX, November, 1950)." See online https://www.vatican .va/content/pius-xii/en/apost_constitutions/documents/hf_p-xii_apc_19501101_ munificentissimus-deus.html.

5. Catholic Catechism, CC# 966 see online https://www.catholiccrossreference .online/catechism/#!/search/s1.2.3.9.6.

6. Rahner, Karl, Mary, Mother of the Lord. *Theological Meditations*. First German edition,1956. Translated by W. J. O'Hara, (New York, NY, Herder and Herder, 1963). See also Rahner, Karl, 1973. *On the Theology of Death*. First German edition, 1947. 1961 English edition translated by C. H. Henkey. Second revised English edition by W. J. O'Hara (New York, NY, The Seabury Press, 1963). See also Rahner, Karl, 2004.

Samtliche Werke, Band 9, Maria, Mutter des Herrn: Mariologische Studien, edited by Regina Pacis Meyer. Freiburg in Breisgau: Herder. This includes the "Editionsbericht" by Meyer (pp. xi–lvi), and Rahner's *Assumptio Beatae Mariae Virginis* (pp. 3–347) and Excursus: *Zur Theologie des Todes* (pp. 348–417). See also online https://www.karlrahnersociety.com/wp-content/uploads/2021/05/Mark-FischerRahners-1951-Work-on-the-Assumption.pdf.

7. Gregory of Tours, *De gloria beatorum martyrum* 4; PL, 71, 708; see also online https://www.catholicculture.org/culture/library/view.cfm?id=469.

8. http://library.mibckerala.org/lms_frame/eBook/THE%20ASSUMPTION%20OF%20MOSES.pdf.

9. https://www.sacred-texts.com/bib/boe/index.htm.

10. Ibid. Ch. 1. f. 3.

11. https://www.newadvent.org/cathen/02006b.htm see also https://www.christianity.com/wiki/church/what-is-the-assumption-of-mary-origins-of-this-catholic-doctrine.html.

Chapter 9

Resurrection of the Body

From the Old Testament to St. Augustine

BIBLICAL BELIEF AND CHURCH TRADITION

The Church Tradition, since the Fourth Lateran Council in 1215 AD, teaches that all men, whether virtuous or vicious, holy or unholy, "will rise again with their own bodies." In the language of the ancient creeds and in our traditional profession of faith, this return to life is called "Resurrection of the Body." It is called this for two reasons: first, since the soul does not die, it cannot be said that it returns to life; second, the rejection of the heretical contention that the Bible implies that by resurrection there is no return to life of the body, but only the rising of the soul from death to life. This is not consistent with either the intended meaning of the Biblical verses or the Tradition of the church. Many of the early heresies stemmed from the teachings of Plato and other philosophers of the time who regarded the body as the prison of the soul and saw death as an escape from the bondage of matter. The Biblical and Traditional belief in the resurrection of the body also combated against the heresies of the Gnostics and the Manicheans who looked upon all matter as evil.

CHURCH TRADITION AND PROFESSIONS OF FAITH

The ancient creeds and continuous profession of faith throughout all the church councils leave no doubt that the Resurrection of the Body is an article of faith. We need look no further than the Apostles' Creed or the Nicene and Athanasian Creeds. For example, the final paragraph of the Apostles' Creed clearly voices this belief:

> I believe in the Holy Spirit,
> the holy Catholic Church,
> the communion of saints,
> the forgiveness of sins,
> the resurrection of the body,
> and life everlasting.
> Amen.[1]

This article of faith as inherent in the continuous Church Tradition is based on the Biblical teachings contained within both the Old Testament and the New Testament.

OLD TESTAMENT SOURCES

In the Old Testament, the history of the Maccabees shows the Jewish belief in the resurrection of the body. Belief in the future resurrection of the body is clearly stated here. For example, in the Book of Maccabees we find the mother of the martyrs voicing the following as she watched her sons in horror:

> I know that He shall rise again, in the resurrection at the last day.

And the Maccabean martyrs putting forth their tongues and stretching out their hands while saying:

> You accursed fiend, you are depriving us of this present life, but the King of the universe will raise us up to live again forever, because we are dying for his laws. —It was from Heaven that I received these; for the sake of his laws, I disregard them; from him I hope to receive them again. (2 Mac. 7:9–11). (See also 12:44; 14:46.)

The Old Testament Apocalyptic Book of Daniel (12:2; cf. 12) also indicates the same belief:

> Many of those that sleep in the dust of the earth, shall awake: some unto life everlasting, and others unto reproach, to see it always. (Dan. 12:2–3, 12)

And finally, Ezekiel's vision of the resurrection of the dry bones refers directly to the restoration of Israel, but such a figure would be hardly intelligible except by those familiar with the belief in a literal and bodily resurrection from the dead:

The hand of the LORD came upon me, and he led me out in the spirit of the LORD and set me in the center of the broad valley. It was filled with bones. He made me walk among them in every direction. So many lay on the surface of the valley! How dry they were! He asked me: "Son of man, can these bones come back to life?" "Lord GOD, I answered, you alone know that." . . . Therefore, prophesy and say to them: Thus says the Lord GOD: Look! I am going to open your graves; I will make you come up out of your graves, my people, and bring you back to the land of Israel. (Eze. 37:1–12)

There are other references to resurrection of the body in the Old Testament in the Book of Isaiah, (25:8; and 26:19–21), The Book of Hosea (6:2), as well as in the Book of Job (19:25–27). [2]

NEW TESTAMENT SOURCES

The resurrection of the dead was expressly taught by Jesus Christ in the Gospels. Here are some examples from the Gospel of John:

Do not be amazed at this, because the hour is coming in which all who are in the tombs will hear his voice and will come out, those who have done good deeds to the resurrection of life, but those who have done wicked deeds to the resurrection of condemnation. (Jn. 5:28–29)

Also

This is the will of the one who sent me, that I should not lose anything of what he gave me, but that I should raise it on the last day. For this is the will of my Father, that everyone who sees the Son and believes in him may have eternal life, and I shall raise him on the last day. (Jn. 6:39–40)

And

Jesus told her, "I am the resurrection and the life; whoever believes in me, even if he dies, will live, and everyone who lives and believes in me will never die. Do you believe this?" (Jn. 11:25–26)

There are further examples of Jesus's Gospel teachings on the resurrection of the dead in both Matthew and Luke (See Mt. 22:29–32 and Lk. 14:14; 20:34–38)

Also in the New Testament, the Apostle Paul will go as far as to place the general resurrection of the dead on the same level of certainty with that of the Resurrection of Jesus Christ:

But if Christ is preached as raised from the dead, how can some among you say there is no resurrection of the dead? If there is no resurrection of the dead, then neither has Christ been raised. And if Christ has not been raised, then empty too is our preaching; empty, too, your faith. Then we are also false witnesses to God because we testified against God that he raised Christ, whom he did not raise if in fact the dead are not raised. For if the dead are not raised, neither has Christ been raised, and if Christ has not been raised, your faith is vain; you are still in your sins. (1 Cor. 15:12–17)

Paul the Apostle preached the resurrection of the dead as one of the fundamental doctrines of the newly formed Christian community. He proclaims this teaching at Athens (see Acts 17:18, 31–32), then at Jerusalem (see Acts 23:6), then before Felix (see Acts 24:15), also before Agrippa (see Acts 26:8). He further proclaims this same teaching on the resurrection of the dead in some of his other New Testament letters such as Romans (see Rom. 6:4–5, 8:11), 2 Corinthians (see 2 Cor. 4:14), Philippians (Phi. 3:21), 1st Thessalonians (1 The. 4:12–16), and 2nd Timothy (2 Tim. 2:11).

EARLY CHURCH FATHERS AS SOURCES

It should come as no surprise that the Tradition of the early Church Fathers agrees with the clear teachings of both the Old and New Testaments. We have already referred to a number of creeds and professions of faith which may be considered as part of the Church's official expression of her faith. Here we have only to point to what the Early Church Fathers teach on the doctrine of the general resurrection in explicit terms. What they have to say is confirmation of the continuous church tradition on the subject. St. Clement of Rome's Letter to the Corinthians was one of the earliest examples:

> Let us consider, beloved, how the Lord continually shows us that there will be a future resurrection; of which he has made our Lord Jesus Christ the first fruits, by raising him from the dead.[3]

Others included St. Justin Martyr (*De Resurrect VII*), Athenagoras (*De Resurrect, Carn. III.*), Tatian (*Adv. Graec.VI*), St. Irenaeus (*Contra Her.*), Tertullian, (*Contra Marcion, De Prescript; On the Resurrection of the Flesh I.12, 15, 63*), Origen (*De Principiis Preface no. 5*), Hippolytus (*Adv. Graec. in P.G., X, 799*) St. Cyril of Jerusalem (*Catechetical Lectures XVIII.15*), St. Ephraem (*De Resurrect. Mort.*), St. Basil *(Ep. CCLXXI, 3)*, St. Ambrose (*De Excessu. frat. sui Satyri, II, lxvii, cii; Idem, In Ps. CXVIII, Serm. X, n. 18; Ps. Ambr., De Trinit*), St. Jerome, (*Ep. ad Paul" in LIII, 8*), St. Chrysostom *(Ps.*

Chrysostom, Fragm. in Libr. Job; in P.G., LXIV, 619) St. Peter Chrysologus, (*Sermon 103, 118; Apostolic Constitutions. XLI*).[4]

Finally, perhaps the greatest of the early Christian Church Fathers and Theologians, The Doctor of Grace, St. Augustine, was given the title, Doctor of Grace for his defense against many church heresies regarding the need for God's grace and our dependence on grace in all things including our future resurrection from the dead and entry unto eternal life.

ST. AUGUSTINE AND RESURRECTION OF THE BODY

"We are an Easter People and Alleluia is our Song."

St. Augustine

Besides St. Paul the Apostle, St. Augustine was perhaps the foremost thinker and theologian in the early Christian church. He was born in Africa in the year 354, became Bishop of Hippo in 396, and died in 430. Among others, his two major theological works were *Confessions* and *The City of God*. It was really Augustine, along with the philosopher Aristotle, who laid the foundation for Christian thinking for Thomas Aquinas in the Middle Ages and ultimately influenced much of Modern Christian thought as well. He is formally recognized as a Doctor of the Church as well as The Doctor of Grace. It is primarily St. Augustine's second major theological work, *City of God*, which has the most to convey regarding Christian belief in both the resurrection of Jesus Christ as well as our own hope-filled promise of a bodily resurrection. In this long theological treatise consisting of twenty-two books, Augustine imagined the Church as a spiritual or Heavenly City of God which was distinct from the material Earthly City. It would be difficult to pinpoint exactly where St Augustine got *City of God* as the title for this work. There are at least 11 references to it in the Scriptures. Many of these are in the Psalms (ex. Ps. 46:4–5, 48:1–3, 87:3), however in my opinion the most likely source might have been these verses in the Book of Revelation as follows:

> Then I saw a new heaven and a new earth. The former heaven and the former earth had passed away, and the sea was no more. I also saw the holy city, a new Jerusalem, coming down out of heaven from God, prepared as a bride adorned for her husband. (Rev. 21:1–2)

City of God was a metaphor for the mystical heavenly city founded on the ordered love of God. The city was seen to be more spiritual than political. Augustine was one of the first Christian authors with a very clear vision of theological- anthropology. This vision extended its influence and reach to

St. Thomas Aquinas in the Middle Ages and then to many of the modern prominent Catholic/Christian theologians of today such as the late Jesuit Karl Rahner, whose theology was called a Transcendental Anthropology or Theological Anthropology. St Augustine gave us an early advance warning of what we would be facing in the spread of Christian belief in the resurrection of the body when he told us:

> No doctrine of the Christian Faith is so vehemently and so obstinately opposed as the doctrine of the resurrection of the flesh.[5]

Augustine saw the human being as a perfect unity of soul and body. He exhorted respect for the body on the grounds it belonged to the very nature of the human person. His favorite figure to describe the body-soul unity was marriage. He saw the love between a man and a woman as hinting at the divine love revealed in the resurrection This perspective on the resurrection was proposed centuries ago by Augustine when he said:

> Give me someone who loves, and they will understand the resurrection.[6]

CITY OF GOD—ST. AUGUSTINE

Among the twenty-two books Augustine left us, the three *City of God* Books which contain the most pertinent Christian thinking on the resurrection of the body are Books XIX, XX, and XXII. Some excerpts from these three Books are as follows:

City of God, Book XIX: The End of the Two Cities

> For in this abode of weakness, and in these wicked days, this state of anxiety has also its use, stimulating us to seek with keener longing for that security where peace is complete and unassailable. There we shall enjoy the gifts of nature, that is to say, all that God the Creator of all natures has bestowed upon ours—gifts not only good, but eternal—not only of the spirit, healed now by wisdom, but also of the body renewed by the resurrection. (*City of God*, Book XIX, Ch. 10)

City of God, Book XX: Concerning the Judgement

> A judgment is to take place, and that it is to take place at the resurrection of the dead . . . the evangelist John most distinctly states that He (Jesus) had predicted that the judgment should be at the resurrection of the dead. (*City of God*, Book XX: Ch. 1–5)

City of God, Book XX: What Is the First Resurrection— What Is the Second?

After that He adds the words, Verily, verily, I say unto you, the hour is coming, and now is, when the dead shall hear the voice of the Son of God; and they that hear shall live. For as the Father has life in Himself; so, has He given to the Son to have life in Himself. John 5:25–26 As yet He does not speak of the second resurrection, that is, the resurrection of the body, which shall be in the end, but of the first, which now is . . . And of this judgment He went on to say, and has given Him authority to execute Judgment, also because He is the Son of man. Here He shows that He will come to judge in that flesh in which He had come to be judged. For it is to show this He says, because He is the Son of man. And then follow the words for our purpose: Marvel not at this: for the hour is coming, in the which all that are in the graves shall hear His voice and shall come forth; they that have done good, unto the resurrection of life; and they that have done evil, unto the resurrection of judgment. John 5:28–29 This judgment He uses here in the same sense as a little before, when He says, He that hears my word, and believes in Him that sent me, has everlasting life, and shall not come into judgment, but is passed from death to life; i.e., by having a part in the first resurrection, by which a transition from death to life is made in this present time, he shall not come into damnation, which He mentions by the name of judgment, as also in the place where He says, but they that have done evil unto the resurrection of judgment, i.e., of damnation. He, therefore, who would not be damned in the second resurrection, let him rise in the first. For the hour is coming, and now is, when the dead shall hear the voice of the Son of God; and they that hear shall live, i.e., shall not come into damnation, which is called the second death; into which death, after the second or bodily resurrection, they shall be hurled who do not rise in the first or spiritual resurrection. For the hour is coming (but here He does not say, and now is, because it shall come in the end of the world in the last and greatest judgment of God) when all that are in the graves shall hear His voice and shall come forth. He does not say, as in the first resurrection, and they that Hear shall live. For all shall not live, at least with such life as ought alone to be called life because it alone is blessed. For some kind of life they must have in order to hear, and come forth from the graves in their rising bodies. And why all shall not live He teaches in the words that follow: They that have done good, to the resurrection of life—these are they who shall live; but they that have done evil, to the resurrection of judgment,—these are they who shall not live, for they shall die in the second death. They have done evil because their life has been evil; and their life has been evil because it has not been renewed in the first or spiritual resurrection which now is, or because they have not persevered to the end in their renewed life. As, then, there are two regenerations, of which I have already made mention—the one according to faith, and which takes place in the present life by means of baptism; the other according to the flesh, and which shall be accomplished in its incorruption and immortality by means of the great and final judgment—so are there also two resurrections—the one the first and spiritual resurrection, which has place in this life, and preserves us from coming into the second death; the other the second, which does not occur now, but in the end of the world, and which is of the body, not of the soul, and which by the last judgment shall dismiss some into the second death, others into that life which has no death. (*City of God*, Book XX: Ch. 6)

City of God, Book XX: What Is the Reign of the Saints with Christ for a Thousand Years, and How it Differs from the Eternal Kingdom

And therefore, when the day of the bodily resurrection arrives, they shall come out of their graves, not to life, but to judgment, namely, to damnation, which is called the second death. For whosoever has not lived until the thousand years be finished, i.e., during this whole time in which the first resurrection is going on— whosoever has not heard the voice of the Son of God and passed from death to life—that man shall certainly in the second resurrection, the resurrection of the flesh, pass with his flesh into the second death. For he goes to say This is the first resurrection. Blessed and holy is he that has part in the first resurrection, or who experiences it. (*City of God*, Book XX: Ch. 9)

City of God, Book XX: After the Resurrection of the Body

Thus, put beyond a doubt that that judgment in which the good and the bad shall be allotted to their destinies shall take place after the resurrection of the body, our faith in which is thoroughly established by the use of these words. (*City of God*, Book XX: Ch. 21)

In another place the same Daniel says, and there shall be a time of trouble, such as was not since there was born a nation upon earth until that time: and in that time all Your people which shall be found written in the book shall be delivered. And many of them that sleep in the mound of earth shall arise, some to everlasting life, and some to shame and everlasting confusion. (*City of God*, Book XX: Ch. 23)

City of God, Book XXII: The End of the City of God

This book treats of the end of the city of God. That is to say, of the eternal happiness of the saints; the faith of the resurrection of the body is established and explained; and the work concludes by showing how the saints, clothed in immortal and spiritual bodies, shall be employed.

It is indubitable that the resurrection of Christ, and His ascension into heaven with the flesh in which He rose, is already preached and believed in the whole world. (*City of God*, Book XXII: Ch. 5)

For if the resurrection of the flesh to eternal life had not taken place in Christ, and were not to be accomplished in His people, as predicted by Christ, or by the prophets who foretold that Christ was to come, why do the martyrs who were slain for this faith which proclaims the resurrection possess such power? . . . finally, some things are done in one way, others in another, and so that man cannot at all comprehend them—nevertheless these miracles attest this faith which preaches the resurrection of the flesh to eternal life. (*City of God*, Book XXII: Ch. 9)

Let us therefore believe those who both speak the truth and work wonders. For by speaking the truth they suffered, and so won the power of working wonders. And the leading truth they professed is that Christ rose from the dead, and first showed in His own flesh the immortality of the resurrection which He promised should be ours, either in the beginning of the world to come, or in the end of this world. (*City of God*, Book XXII: Ch. 10)

The woman, therefore, is a creature of God even as the man; but by her creation from man unity is commended; and the manner of her creation prefigured, as has been said, Christ and the Church. He, then, who created both sexes will restore both. (*City of God*, Book XXII: Ch. 17)

If it is contended that each will rise with the same stature as that of the body he died in, we shall not obstinately dispute this, provided only there be no deformity, no infirmity, no languor, no corruption—nothing of any kind which would ill become that kingdom in which the children of the resurrection and of the promise shall be equal to the angels of God, if not in body and age, at least in happiness. *(City of God*, Book XXII: Ch. 20)

But there is not now space to treat of these ages; suffice it to say that the seventh shall be our Sabbath, which shall be brought to a close, not by an evening, but by the Lord's day as an eighth and eternal day, consecrated by the resurrection of Christ, and prefiguring the eternal repose not only of the spirit, but also of the body. There we shall rest and see, see and love, love and praise . . . I think I have now, by God's help, discharged my obligation in writing this large work. Let those who think I have said too little, or those who think I have said too much, forgive me; and let those who think I have said just enough join me in giving thanks to God. Amen. (*City of God*, Book XXII: Ch. 30)[7]

As we move ahead in the next chapter from St Augustine to St Thomas Aquinas, we will find that they both agree on many things Christian, including that the soul and the body are distinct. But only Aquinas in his theology and philosophy will firmly maintain early on that there is no possibility for happiness or bliss unless the soul is unified with the body as one being composed of body and soul. To Aquinas, the body and soul are ultimately inseparable. In his understanding of the nature of Jesus Christ, Thomas

Aquinas maintained that Christ had a real body of the same nature of ours, a true rational soul, and, together with these, formed a perfect Deity. This will set the stage for more modern Christian theological constructs such as Jesuit Karl Rahner's Theological Anthropology or Transcendental Anthropology which will attempt to explore resurrection of the body by using a modern theological-philosophical approach similarly to Thomas Aquinas. But Rahner will ground his theology in the human person and his or her orientation to the transcendent God of the universe and the grace of God's self-communication.[8]

NOTES

1. Apostles Creed, United Conference of Catholic Bishops, UCCB, online https://www.usccb.org/prayers/apostles-creed.
2. Ibid. Ch. 1, f. 3.
3. Clement of Rome, Letter to the Corinthians, Ch.11: 16–18.
4. St. Justin Martyr (De Resurrect VII)., Athenagoras (De Resurrect, Carn. III.), Tatian (Adv. Graec.VI), St. Irenaeus (Contra Her.), Tertullian, (Contra Marcion, De Prescript; On the Resurrection of the Flesh I.12, 15, 63), Origen (De Principiis Preface no. 5), Hippolytus (Adv. Graec. in P.G., X, 799) St. Cyril of Jerusalem (Catechetical Lectures XVIII.15), St. Ephraem (De Resurrect. Mort.), St. Basil (Ep. CCLXXI, 3), St. Ambrose (De Excessu. frat. sui Satyri, II, lxvii, cii; Idem, In Ps. CXVIII, Serm. X, n. 18; Ps. Ambr., De Trinit), St. Jerome, (Ep. ad Paul" in LIII, 8), St. Chrysostom (Ps. Chrysostom, Fragm. in Libr. Job; in P.G., LXIV, 619) St. Peter Chrysologus, (Sermon 103, 118; Apostolic Constitutions. XLI).
5. St. Augustine (In Ps. LXXXVIII, Sermon II, no. 5).
6. Gerald O'Collins, *What Are They Saying About the Resurrection?* (New York, NY, Paulist Press,: 1978). See also http://www.nationalcatholicreporter.org/sanchez/locked/cyclea/eastera/easter196a.htm.
7. New Advent Catholic Encyclopedia online version St. Augustine and the subject "Resurrection of the Body." APA citation. Maas, A. (1911). General Resurrection. In *The Catholic Encyclopedia*. New York: Robert Appleton Company. Retrieved October 19, 2022 from New Advent: http://www.newadvent.org/cathen/12792a.htm. MLA citation. Maas, Anthony. "General Resurrection." The Catholic Encyclopedia. Vol. 12. New York: Robert Appleton Company, 1911. 19 Oct. 2022; http://www.newadvent.org/cathen/12792a.htm.https://www.newavent.org/cathen/12792a.htm. See also https://thoughtfulcatholic.com/?p=46952Ott, Ludwig. *Fundamentals of Catholic Dogma*. Edited by James Canon Bastible, DD, translated by Patrick Lynch, Rockford, IL, TAN Books and Publishers, Inc., 1955.
8. Ibid. Ch. 10 and Ch. 11.

Chapter 10

The *Summa* of St. Thomas Aquinas and the Resurrection of the Body

ST. THOMAS AQUINAS

St. Thomas Aquinas, The Angelic Doctor of the Church, was born in Sicily in 1274. He became a Dominican priest and was the foremost theologian and scholastic of the Middle Ages. His theology relied heavily on the philosophy of Aristotle, especially in the areas of Metaphysics, Ethics, Providence, Resurrection, Creation and Anthropology. Aquinas in his theology, repeatedly referred to Aristotle as "the Philosopher" as he attempted to synthesize Aristotelian philosophy with the principal truths contained in the Christian religion. Whenever the philosophy of Aristotle came into conflict with Christian belief, Thomas never compromised the truths of Christianity and always modified Aristotle's philosophy instead. He was a very prolific theologian, but his major theological work was *The Summa Theologica* which was a classically systemized theology. Aquinas was a proponent of natural theology and the father of a school of thought which encompassed both theology and philosophy known as Thomism. St Thomas Aquinas influenced many modern Catholic/Christian theologians including the Theological Anthropology of Jesuit Karl Rahner which is sometimes referred to as "Transcendental Thomism." Rahner's theology will be discussed particularly as it relates to resurrection of the body in Chapter 11, the next chapter of this book.

Thomas maintained that a human person is a single material substance. He understood the soul to be the form of the body which makes a human being the composite of the two. Thomas envisioned faith and reason, while distinct, to be the two primary tools for processing the data of theology.

In his theology, he argued that God is simultaneously both the source of the light of natural reason and the light of faith. In his understanding of the nature of Jesus Christ, Thomas Aquinas maintained that Christ's real body and truly rational soul formed a perfect Deity. Thus, there is both unity (hypostasis) and composition in the two natures of Jesus Christ—human and divine. Aquinas identified the goal of human existence as complete, loving, and eternal union with God. This could only be achieved through the beatific vision, in which a person experiences perfect and never-ending happiness by seeing God face to face. The vision occurs after human death and resurrection as the gift and grace of God given to those who, in life, experienced salvation and redemption through Christ.

In much of his theology on the resurrection, Thomas Aquinas argued that the soul persists after the death and corruption of the body and is capable of an existence between the time of death and the resurrection of the flesh. Resurrection is an important part of his philosophy and theology concerning the soul. The human person is seen as fulfilled and complete in the body, so the hereafter must consist of the soul in the matter of a resurrected body. In addition to the hope of spiritual reward promised in eternity, humans can expect to enjoy material and physical blessings as well. Because Thomas's theology of the resurrected soul requires a body for its actions, during the afterlife, the soul will also be punished or rewarded in bodily existence. However, all reward is purely through the grace of God.[1]

ST. THOMAS AQUINAS ON THE
BODY OF THE RISEN CHRIST

In his *Summa*, Thomas Aquinas maintained that, after the resurrection of Christ, the same body, for which his soul had been the form before his death, was once again united with his soul. Because the truth of the nature of the body is from the form (i.e., the soul), it follows that the body of Christ after the resurrection would be a real, albeit glorified, spiritized body and of the same nature as before.

According to Aquinas, the body of the risen Christ was "integral" and therefore included flesh, bones, blood, etc., and was of the same nature as before death, although it was now glorified and incorruptible, as well as being no longer subject to death. Aquinas also considered it appropriate that the body, which the soul of Christ again took on in the resurrection, had the wounds and scars suffered in the crucifixion and passion. On the other hand, it was now "spiritual," and that body was real and solid, could be touched and seen, and was able to eat and drink. Aquinas maintained that it is through the soul that the body becomes a being in action. Therefore, the soul is the form of the animated body.[2] There are several sections of Thomas' *Summa* that relate to his theology on the resurrection of Jesus Christ as well as the bodily resurrection of human persons. For us, the resurrection of the body is an event in the future, and our knowledge can only be drawn from revelation and our understanding of our Lord's resurrection. What follows are some of the questions and answers, particularly those on the unity of body and soul, Thomas posed on resurrection in his *Summa Theologica*. Because all of them taken together would make up an entire book in themselves, we are limited as to how many of his questions and answers will be presented here. I have selected those which I feel are the most pertinent to bodily resurrection and those in particular which would have a bearing on more modern theologies such as the theology of Jesuit, Karl Rahner.

THE *SUMMA THEOLOGICA* OF THOMAS AQUINAS ON RESURRECTION OF THE BODY

Question 75: Article 1

Is There to Be a Resurrection of the Body?

I answer that, according to the various opinions about man's last end; there have been various opinions holding or denying the resurrection. For man's last end which all men desire naturally is happiness. Some have held that man is able to attain this end in this life; wherefore they had no need to admit another life after this, wherein man would be able to attain to his perfection, and so they denied the resurrection.

This opinion is confuted with sufficient probability by the changeableness of fortune, the weakness of the human body, the imperfection and instability of knowledge and virtue, all of which are hindrances to the perfection of happiness, as Augustine argues at the end of *De Civ. Dei* (xxii, 22).

Hence, others maintained that after this there is another life wherein, after death, man lives according to the soul only, and they held that such a life sufficed to satisfy the natural desire to obtain happiness: wherefore Porphyrius said as Augustine states (*De Civ. De.* xxii, 26): "The soul, to be happy, must avoid all bodies": and consequently, these did not hold the resurrection.

This opinion was based by various people on various false foundations. For certain heretics asserted that all bodily things are from the evil principle, but that spiritual things are from the good principle. From this it follows that the soul cannot reach the height of its perfection unless it be separated from the body, since the latter withdraws it from its principle, the participation of which makes it happy. Hence all those heretical sects that hold corporeal things to have been created or fashioned by the devil deny the resurrection of the body. The falsehood of this principle has been shown at the beginning of the Second Book (Sent. ii, D, 4, qu. 1, 3; * [Cf. I:49:3]).

Others said that the entire nature of man is seated in the soul, so that the soul makes use of the body as an instrument, or as a sailor uses his ship. According to this opinion, it follows that if happiness is attained by the soul alone, man would not be balked in his natural desire for happiness, and so there is no need to hold the resurrection. The Philosopher sufficiently destroys this foundation (*De Anima* ii, 2), where he shows that the soul is united to the body as form to matter. Hence it is clear that if man cannot be happy in this life, we must of necessity hold the resurrection.

Question 75: Article 2

Whether The Resurrection Will Be for All Without Exception?

I answer that those things, the reason of which comes from the nature of a species, must needs be found likewise in all the members of that same species. Now such is the resurrection: because the reason thereof, as stated above (Article 1) is that the soul cannot have the final perfection of the human species, so long as it is separated from the body. Hence no soul will remain forever separated from the body. Therefore, it is necessary for all, as well as for one, to rise again.

Question 75: Article 3

Whether the Resurrection Is Natural?

I answer that, a movement or an action stands related to nature in three ways. For there is a movement or action whereof nature is neither the principle nor the term: and such a movement is sometimes from a principle above nature as in the case of a glorified body. Sometimes from any other principle whatever— for instance, the violent upward movement of a stone which terminates in a violent rest . . .

In nature there is no active principle of the resurrection, neither as regards the union of the soul with the body, nor as regards the disposition which is the demand for that union since such a disposition cannot be produced by nature, except in a definite way by the process of generation from seed. Even granted a passive potentiality on the part of the body or any kind of inclination to its union with the soul, it is not such as to suffice for the conditions of natural movement. Therefore, the resurrection, strictly speaking, is miraculous and not natural except in a restricted sense, as we have explained.[3]

Question 76: The Union of Body and Soul

*Article 1: Whether the Intellectual Principle Is United to the
Body as its Form?*

I answer that we must assert that the intellect which is the principle of intellectual operation is the form of the human body . . . There remains, therefore, no
other explanation than that given by Aristotle—namely, that this particular man
understands, because the intellectual principle is his form. Thus, from the very
operation of the intellect it is made clear that the intellectual principle is united
to the body as its form.

Question 76: Article 5

*Whether the Intellectual Soul Is Properly United to Such
a Body?*

I answer that, Since the form is not for the matter, but rather the matter for the
form, we must gather from the form the reason why the matter is such as it is;
and not conversely. Now the intellectual soul, as we have seen above (I:55:2)
in the order of nature, holds the lowest place among intellectual substances;
inasmuch as it is not naturally gifted with the knowledge of truth, as the angels
are; but has to gather knowledge from individual things by way of the senses, as
Dionysius says (*Div. Nom.* vii). But nature never fails in necessary things. The
intellectual soul had to be endowed not only with the power of understanding,
but also with the power of feeling. Now the action of the senses is not performed
without a corporeal instrument. Therefore, it behooved the intellectual soul to be
united to a body fitted to be a convenient organ of sense.

Now all the other senses are based on the sense of touch. The organ of touch
requires to be a medium between contraries, such as hot and cold, wet and dry,
and the like, of which the sense of touch has the perception; thus it is in potentiality with regard to contraries and is able to perceive them. Therefore, the more
the organ of touch is reduced to an equable complexion, the more sensitive will
be the touch. The intellectual soul has the power of sense in all its complete-
ness because what belongs to the inferior nature pre-exists more perfectly in the
superior, as Dionysius says (*Div. Nom.* v).

Therefore, the body to which the intellectual soul is united should be a mixed
body, above others reduced to the most equable complexion. For this reason,
among animals, man has the best sense of touch. Among men, those who have
the best sense of touch have the best intelligence, a sign of which is that we
observe "those who are refined in body are well endowed in mind" as stated in
Aristotle, *De Anima* ii, 9.[4]

Question 77: Article 1

Should the Time of the Resurrection Be Delayed Until the End of the World?

I answer that, as Augustine states (*De Trin.* iii, 4) "Divine providence decreed that the grosser and lower bodies should be ruled in a certain order by the more subtle and powerful bodies." The entire matter of the lower bodies is subject to variation according to the movement of the heavenly bodies. Hence it would be contrary to the order established in things by Divine providence if the matter of lower bodies were brought to the state of incorruption, so long as there remains movement in the higher bodies. Since, according to the teaching of faith, the resurrection will bring men to immortal life conformably to Christ who "rising again from the dead dieth now no more" (Romans 6:9), the resurrection of human bodies will be delayed until the end of the world when the heavenly movement will cease. For this reason, too, certain philosophers, who held that the movement of the heavens will never cease, maintained that human souls will return to mortal bodies such as we have now—whether, as Empedocles, they stated that the soul would return to the same body at the end of the great year, or that it would return to another body; thus Pythagoras asserted that "any soul will enter any body," as stated in *De Anima* i, 3.[5]

Question 79: Article 1

Will the Body Rise Again Identically the Same?

I answer that, on this point, the philosophers erred and certain modern heretics err. Some of the philosophers allowed that souls separated from bodies are reunited to bodies, yet they erred in this in two ways. First, as to the mode of reunion, for some held the separated soul to be naturally reunited to a body by the way of generation. Secondly, as to the body to which it was reunited, for they held that this second union was not with the selfsame body that was laid aside in death, but with another, sometimes of the same, sometimes of a different species. Of a different species, when the soul while existing in the body had led a life contrary to the ordering of reason, wherefore it passed after death from the body of a man into the body of some other animal to whose manner of living it had conformed in this life, for instance into the body of a dog on account of lust, into the body of a lion on account of robbery and violence, and so forth—and into a body of the same species when the soul has led a good life in the body, and having after death experienced some happiness, after some centuries began to wish to return to the body, and thus it was reunited to a human body.

This opinion arises from two false sources. The first of these is that they said that the soul is not united to the body essentially as form to matter, but only accidentally, as mover to the thing moved, [Cf. I:76:1] or as a man to his clothes. Hence it was possible for them to maintain that the soul pre-existed before being infused into the body begotten of natural generation, as also that it is united to various bodies. The second is that they held intellect not to differ from sense except accidentally, so that man would be said to surpass other animals in intelligence because the sensitive power is more acute in him on account of the excellence of his bodily complexion. Hence it was possible for them to assert that man's soul passes into the soul of a brute animal, especially when the human soul has been habituated to brutish actions. These two sources are refuted by the Philosopher (*De Anima* ii, 1), and in consequence of these being refuted, it is clear that the above opinion is false.

In like manner the errors of certain heretics are refuted. Some of them fell into the aforesaid opinions of the philosophers, while others held that souls are reunited to heavenly bodies, or again to bodies subtle as the wind, as Gregory relates of a certain Bishop of Constantinople in his exposition of Job 19:26, "In my flesh I shall see my God," etc. Moreover, these same errors of heretics may be refuted by the fact that they are prejudicial to the truth of resurrection as witnessed to by Holy Writ. For we cannot call it resurrection unless the soul return to the same body, since resurrection is a second rising, and the same thing rises that falls: wherefore resurrection regards the body which after death falls rather than the soul which after death lives. Consequently, if it be not the same body which the soul resumes, it will not be a resurrection, but rather the assuming of a new body.

Question 79: Article 2

Will It Be Identically the Same Man That Shall Rise Again?

I answer that, the necessity of holding the resurrection arises from this—that man may obtain the last end for which he was made; for this cannot be accomplished in this life, nor in the life of the separated soul as stated above (*Supplement*:75:2), otherwise, man would have been made in vain, if he were unable to obtain the end for which he was made. Since it behooves the end to be obtained by the selfsame thing that was made for that end, lest it appear to be made without purpose, it is necessary for the selfsame man to rise again; and this is effected by the selfsame soul being united to the selfsame body. Otherwise there would be no resurrection properly speaking, if the same man were not reformed. Hence, to maintain that he who rises again is not the selfsame man is heretical, since it is contrary to the truth of Scripture which proclaims the resurrection.[6]

Question 53: Article 4

Was Christ the Cause of His Own Resurrection?

I answer that, as stated above (III:50:3), in consequence of death, Christ's Godhead was not separated from His soul nor from His flesh. Consequently, both the soul and the flesh of the dead Christ can be considered in two respects: first, in respect of His Godhead; secondly, in respect of His created nature. Therefore, according to the virtue of the Godhead united to it, the body took back again the soul which it had laid aside, and the soul took back again the body which it had abandoned, and thus Christ rose by His own power. This is precisely what is written (2 Corinthians 13:4): "For although He was crucified through" our "weakness, yet He liveth by the power of God." If we consider the body and soul of the dead Christ according to the power of created nature, they could not thus be reunited, but it was necessary for Christ to be raised up by God.[7]

Question 54: Article 1

Did Christ Have a True Body After His Resurrection?

I answer that, as Damascene says (*De Fide Orth.* iv), that is said to rise, which fell. Christ's body fell by death; namely, inasmuch as the soul which was its formal perfection was separated from it. Hence, in order for it to be a true resurrection, it was necessary for the same body of Christ to be once more united with the same soul. Since the truth of the body's nature is from its form it follows that Christ's body after His Resurrection was a true body and of the same nature as it was before, but had His been an imaginary body, then His Resurrection would not have been true, but apparent.

Question 54: Article 2

Did Christ's Body Rise Glorified?

I answer that Christ's was a glorified body in His Resurrection, and this is evident for three reasons. First of all, because His Resurrection was the exemplar and the cause of ours, as is stated in 1 Corinthians 15:43. In the resurrection, the saints will have glorified bodies, as is written in the same place, "It is sown in dishonor, it shall rise in glory." Hence, since the cause is mightier than the effect, and the exemplar than the exemplate, much more glorious, then, was the body of Christ in His Resurrection. Secondly, because He merited the glory of His Resurrection by the lowliness of His Passion. Hence, He said (John 12:27): "Now is My soul troubled," which refers to the Passion; and later He adds: "Father, glorify Thy name," whereby He asks for the glory of the Resurrection. Thirdly, because as stated above (III:34:4), Christ's soul was glorified from the instant of His conception by perfect fruition of the Godhead. As stated above (III:14:1 ad 2), it was owing to the Divine economy that the glory did not pass from His soul to His body in order that by the Passion He might accomplish the mystery of our redemption. Consequently, when this mystery of Christ's Passion and death was finished, straightway the soul communicated its glory to the risen body in the Resurrection and so that body was made glorious.

Question 54: Article 3.

Whether Christ's Body Rose Again Entire?

I answer that as stated above (Article 2), Christ's body in the Resurrection was "of the same nature, but differed in glory." Accordingly, whatever goes with the nature of a human body was entirely in the body of Christ when He rose again. Now it is clear that flesh, bones, blood, and other such things are of the very nature of the human body. Consequently, all these things were in Christ's body when He rose again; and this also integrally, without any diminution, otherwise, it would not have been a complete resurrection if whatever was lost by death had not been restored. Hence our Lord assured His faithful ones by saying (Matthew 10:30): "The very hairs of your head are all numbered": and (Luke 21:18): "A hair of your head shall not perish."

To say that Christ's body had neither flesh, nor bones, nor the other natural parts of a human body, belongs to the error of Eutyches, Bishop of Constantinople, who maintained that "our body in that glory of the resurrection will be impalpable, and more subtle than wind and air, and that our Lord, after the hearts of the disciples who handled Him were confirmed, brought back to subtlety whatever could be handled in Him" [St. Gregory, Moral. in Job 14:56]. Now Gregory condemns this in the same book, because Christ's body was not changed after the Resurrection, according to Romans 6:9: "Christ rising from the dead, dieth now no more." Accordingly, the very man who had said these things, himself retracted them at his death. For, if it be unbecoming for Christ to take a body of another nature in His conception, a heavenly one for instance, as Valentine asserted, it is much more unbecoming for Him at His Resurrection to resume a body of another nature because in His Resurrection He resumed unto an everlasting life, the body which in His conception He had assumed to a mortal life.

Question 54: Article 4

Did Christ's Body Rise with Its Scars?

I answer that it was fitting for Christ's soul at His Resurrection to resume the body with its scars. In the first place, for Christ's own glory. For Bede says on Luke 24:40 that He kept His scars not from inability to heal them, "but to wear them as an everlasting trophy of His victory." Hence Augustine says (*De Civ. Dei* xxii): 'Perhaps in that kingdom we shall see on the bodies of the Martyrs the traces of the wounds which they bore for Christ's name, because it will not be a deformity, but a dignity in them; and a certain kind of beauty will shine in them, in the body, though not of the body.' Secondly, to confirm the hearts of the disciples as to 'the faith in His Resurrection' (Bede, on Luke 24:40). Thirdly, 'that when He pleads for us with the Father, He may always show the manner of death He endured for us' (Bede, on Luke 24:40). Fourthly, 'that He may convince those redeemed in His blood, how mercifully they have been helped, as He exposes before them the traces of the same death' (Bede, on Luke 24:40). Lastly, 'that in the Judgment-day He may upbraid them with their just condemnation' (Bede, on Luke 24:40). Hence, as Augustine says (*De Symb*. ii): 'Christ knew why He kept the scars in His body. For, as He showed them to Thomas who would not believe except he handled and saw them, so will He show His wounds to His enemies, so that He who is the Truth may convict them, saying: 'Behold the man whom you crucified; see the wounds you inflicted; recognize the side you pierced, since it was opened by you and for you, yet you would not enter.'"[8]

Question 56: Article 1

Is Christ's Resurrection the Cause of the Resurrection of Our Bodies?

I answer that as stated in 2 Metaphysics, text 4: 'Whatever is first in any order is the cause of all that come after it.' But Christ's Resurrection was the first in the order of our resurrection, as is evident from what was said above (III:53:3). Hence, Christ's Resurrection must be the cause of ours: and this is what the Apostle says (1 Corinthians 15:20–21): "Christ is risen from the dead, the first-fruits of them that sleep; for by a man came death, and by a man the resurrection of the dead."

This is reasonable because the principle of human life-giving is the Word of God, of whom it is said (Psalm 35:10): 'With Thee is the fountain of life,' hence He Himself says (John 5:21): 'As the Father raiseth up the dead, and giveth life; so the Son also giveth life to whom He will.' Now the divinely established natural order is that every cause operates first upon what is nearest to it, and through it upon others which are more remote; just as fire first heats the nearest air, and through it heats bodies that are further off: and God Himself first enlightens those substances which are closer to Him, and through them others that are more remote, as Dionysius says (*Coel. Hier*. xiii). Consequently, the Word of God first bestows immortal life upon that body which is naturally united with Himself, and through it works the resurrection in all other bodies. Because He is the Son of Man (John 5:27); the efficient power of His Resurrection extends to the good and wicked alike, who are subject to His judgment.

Just as the Resurrection of Christ's body, through its personal union with the Word is first in point of time, so also is it first in dignity and perfection as the gloss says on 1 Corinthians 15:20–23. Whatever is most perfect is always the exemplar, which the less perfect copies according to its mode. Consequently, Christ's Resurrection is the exemplar of ours. This is necessary, not on the part of Him who rose again, who needs no exemplar, but on the part of them who are raised up, who must be likened to that Resurrection, according to Philippians 3:21: 'He will reform the body of our lowness, made like to the body of His glory.' Now although the efficiency of Christ's Resurrection extends to the resurrection of the good and wicked alike, still its exemplarity extends properly only to the just, who are made conformable with His Sonship, according to Romans 8:29.

Question 56: Article 2

Is Christ's Resurrection the Cause of the Resurrection of Souls?

I answer that as stated above, Christ's Resurrection works in virtue of the Godhead. Now this virtue extends not only to the resurrection of bodies, but also to that of souls, for it comes of God that the soul lives by grace, and that the body lives by the soul. Consequently, Christ's Resurrection has instrumentally an effective power not only with regard to the resurrection of bodies, but also with respect to the resurrection of souls. In like fashion it is an exemplar cause with regard to the resurrection of souls, because even in our souls we must be conformed with the rising Christ: as the Apostle says (Romans 6:4–11) 'Christ is risen from the dead by the glory of the Father, so we also may walk in newness of life' and as He, 'rising again from the dead, dieth now no more, so let us reckon that we (Vulgate: 'you')" are dead to sin, that we may 'live together with Him.'"[9]

CHARACTERISTICS OF THE RISEN BODY

All shall rise from the dead in their own, in their entire, and in immortal bodies, but the good shall rise to the resurrection of life, the wicked to the resurrection of Judgment. It would destroy the very idea of resurrection if the dead were to rise in bodies not their own. Again, the resurrection, like the creation, is to be numbered amongst the principal works of God. Hence, as at the creation all things are perfect from the hand of God, so at the resurrection all things must be perfectly restored by the same omnipotent hand. There is a difference between the earthly and the risen body, for the risen bodies of both saints and sinners shall be invested with immortality. This admirable restoration of nature is the result of the glorious triumph of Christ over death as described in several texts of Sacred Scripture: Isaiah 25:8; Osee, xiii, 14; 1 Corinthians 15:26; Apocalypse 2:4. While the just shall enjoy an endless felicity in the entirety of their restored members, the wicked 'shall seek death, and shall not find it, shall desire to die, and death shall fly from them' (Revelation 9:6).

These three characteristics (identity, entirety, and immortality) will be common to the risen bodies of the just and the wicked. But the bodies of the saints shall be distinguished by four transcendent endowments, often called qualities. The first is "IMPASSIBILITY," which shall place them beyond the reach of pain and inconvenience. 'It is sown," says the Apostle, 'in corruption, it shall rise in incorruption' (1 Corinthians 15:42). The Schoolmen call this quality impassibility,' not incorruption, so as to mark it as a peculiarity of the glorified body; the bodies of the damned will be incorruptible indeed, but not impassible; they shall be subject to heat and cold, and all manner of pain. The next quality is "BRIGHTNESS," or "GLORY," by which the bodies of the saints shall shine like the sun. 'It is sown in dishonor,' says the Apostle, 'it shall rise in glory' (1 Corinthians 15:43; cf. Matthew 13:43; 17:2; Philippians 3:21). All the bodies of the saints shall be equally impassible, but they shall be endowed with different degrees of glory. According to St. Paul: 'One is the glory of the sun, another the glory of the moon, another the glory of the stars. For star differs from star in glory'(1 Corinthians 15:41–42).

The third quality is that of "AGILITY," by which the body shall be freed from its slowness of motion, and endowed with the capability of moving with the utmost facility and quickness wherever the soul pleases. The Apostle says: "It is sown in weakness it shall rise in power" (1 Corinthians 15:43). The fourth quality is "SUBTLETY," by which the body becomes subject to the absolute dominion of the soul. This is inferred from the words of the Apostle: 'It is sown a natural body, it shall rise a spiritual body' (1 Corinthians 15:44). The body participates in the soul's more perfect and spiritual life to such an extent that it becomes itself like a spirit. We see this quality exemplified in the fact that Christ passed through material objects."[10]

Jesuit Karl Rahner's modern theology which follows in the next chapter is more popularly called "Theological Anthropology." However, in that Karl Rahner has often been referred to as the "Modern Thomas Aquinas," his theology is occasionally referred to as "Transcendental Thomism." We will find this to be the case particularly as Rahner's theology treats the hope-filled promise of Resurrection of the Body.

NOTES

1. https://www.britannica.com/biography/Saint-Thomas-Aquinas; see also https://www.thomasaquinas.edu/sites/default/files/2022-04/Napa-2022-reading.pdf; see also https://thoughtfulcatholic.com/?p=46952.

2. Thomas Aquinas, *Summa Theologica*, Question 54, Art. 1.

3. Thomas Aquinas, *Summa Theologica,* Online edition 1/3/23 Question 75, Art. 1, 2, and 3. See online https://www.newadvent.org/summa/5075.htm.

4. Ibid. Ch. 12, f.3, Question 76, Art. 1 and 5. https://www.newadvent.org/summa/5076.htm.

5. Ibid. Ch. 12, f.3, Question 77, Art. 1. https://www.newadvent.org/summa/5077 .htm.

6. Ibid. Ch. 12, f. 3, Question 79, Art. 1 and 2. https://www.newadvent.org/summa /5079.htm

7. Ibid. Ch. 12, f. 3, Question 53, Art. 4. https://www.newadvent.org/summa/4053 .htm

8. Ibid. Ch. 12, f. 3, Question 54, Art. 1. 2, 3, and 4. https://www.newadvent.org/ summa/4054.htm.

9. Ibid. Ch. 12, f. 3. Question 56, Art. 1 and 2. https://www.newadvent.org/summa /4056.htm.

10. https://www.newadvent.org/summa/1.htm; see also Maas, Anthony. "General Resurrection." *The Catholic Encyclopedia.* Vol. 12. New York: Robert Appleton Company, 1911. 19 Oct. 2022 http://www.newadvent.org/cathen/12792a.htm. https: //www.newadvent.org/cathen/12792a.htm. Ott, Ludwig. *Fundamentals of Catholic Dogma.* Edited by James Canon Bastible, DD, translated by Patrick Lynch, Rockford, IL, TAN Books and Publishers, Inc., 1955. https://www.catholicdigest.com/amp/from -the-magazine/ask-father/what-is-a-glorified-body/; https://www.encyclopedia.com/ religion/encyclopedias-almanacs-transcripts-and-maps/glorified-body.

Chapter 11

Karl Rahner's Theology—and Resurrection of the Body

KARL RAHNER'S THEOLOGY

The first time I heard the name "Karl Rahner" was when I began my course work for an M-Div. at Weston/The Boston College School of Theology and Ministry. For those of you old enough to remember watching TV in the 1950s, I thought the instructor might have been talking about a comedic actor whose name was actually Karl Reiner, who had a very different persona than Karl Rahner and starred with Sid Caesar and Imogene Coca in the TV Comedy Series, "Show of Shows."[1]

The late Jesuit, Karl Rahner (d. 1984), has often been referred to as the most brilliant Catholic-Christian theologian since Thomas Aquinas. He was one of the theological experts at the Second Vatican Council in 1965—a council which was greatly influenced by Rahner's theology and his understanding of the Catholic faith. He has reshaped modern theology more than any figure ever since the days of Vatican Council II, becoming the most influential theologian of the 20th Century. In his lifetime, Rahner had published almost 4,000 books, essays, dictionaries, and encyclopedias, extending his intellectual reach and articulately expressing his understanding of Catholic/Christian theology and philosophic thought to thousands of Catholic and Protestant scholars alike. A good summary of his theology can be found in his massive four-volume theological encyclopedia, *Sacramentum Mundi,* combined with his three- inch-thick theological handbook, *Foundations of Christian Faith.*[2] Most Catholic scholars, especially those who have pursued theological degrees would not be able to avoid tripping over Father Rahner's words thousands of times in almost every graduate theology course taken during the years of their formation.

Rahner's theology has often been referred to as both "Transcendental Anthropology" and "Theological Anthropology," as it correlated and attempted to systematize the historical experience of the human person and God's grace-filled self-communication. The classic definition of "theology" was described long ago by St. Anselm as "Faith seeking understanding."[3] In his Encyclopedia of Theology, *Sacramentum Mundi,* Rahner defines "anthropology" as "Man's explanation of himself and the reflection on his own being which is always presented as a question." He has also said: "The notion of 'transcendence' derives from experience, i.e., man's experience of going beyond himself, and in relation to God and God's self-communication to man. This is a way of seeing transcendence as "grace."[4] Grace is also very important in Rahner's theology. For him, grace is God's self-communication. The term 'self-communication,' as Rahner uses the term, is really intended to signify that God in his own reality makes himself the innermost constitutive element of man. God's self-communication means that what is communicated IS really God in his own being and reality without ceasing to be absolute Mystery. The giver, in his own being, is the gift— that in and through his own being, the giver (God) gives himself to man as his own fulfillment. In this way, God is communicated to what is not infinite or divine for the sake of knowing God in love.[5]

To Karl Rahner, God is always defined as "Holy Mystery," and it is mystery which is the ground of reality. Nature presupposes and is always confronted by the offer of grace. However, we must always keep in mind that, although Rahner doesn't say so every time in his writings, for him, grace is always Christ's grace— implying that his intended meaning is that it is the grace that comes from the cross and resurrection of Jesus Christ. Therefore, in his theology, Rahner also proposed that there existed what he called, "Anonymous Christians." Christianity, he argued, cannot recognize any other religion as providing the way to salvation. Jesus remains as the only way to the Father. However, since God is love and desires everyone to be saved, God can apply the saving action of Jesus's atoning death and resurrection to everyone. This could include those who have never heard of Jesus, or his death and resurrection, or even those who have never acknowledged Jesus as Son of God and Lord of the universe.[6] We are responsible for who is our final irrevocable self at the end of our earthly sojourn. However, any one person's salvation is ultimately in God's hands.

Rahner refers to the human person's capacity for receiving the grace of God, as the "Supernatural Existential."[7] As a Jesuit, Rahner fell back on his Ignation spirituality in an attempt to "find God in all things." Rahner sought to maintain the traditional teachings of the Church, but to describe them in contemporary terms. In addition to his being thoroughly acquainted with the Bible and Church Tradition throughout the ages, the prominent philosophers,

Marechal, Kant, Hegel, and Heidegger also had tremendous influences on both his philosophy and theology. Karl Rahner became adept at then weaving a philosophical/ theological mosaic from the thinking of all of these men and combined some of their thinking with the theology of Thomas Aquinas (particularly *Summa* 1, Q. 76 on how the soul is united to the body) to arrive at a vibrant synthesis and a systematized theology which today is called both "Theological Anthropology" and "Transcendental Anthropology."[8]

RAHNER ON BODY, SOUL, AND SPIRIT

As we move toward a discussion of Karl Rahner's theology on the Resurrection of the Body, we should try to get at an understanding of his definition of the terms, body, soul, and spirit. Like Thomas Aquinas before him, in his theology Rahner maintained that it is through the physicality of the body that the united soul interacts with the world and not in any dualistic manner; soul and body, spirit and matter are united and inseparable. Rahner consistently prefers the term "spirit" over the word "soul." When Rahner uses the word "spirit," he is sometimes philosophically referencing the human person's disposition over and against the world where all matter is oriented toward spirit. God is pure Spirit and what is material is always oriented toward the spiritual. When he uses the word "soul," he is speaking of the soul united to the physicality of the "body" (not dualistically) interacting with the world and theologically asserting the ultimate orientation of the spiritized body toward God in Christ.

Perhaps, it might be helpful at this point to turn to Karl Rahner's Theological Encyclopedia to look at his concise definitions of the terms, "body," "soul," and "spirit." In speaking about the body in his *Sacramentum Mundi*, Encyclopedia of Theology, Rahner states the following:

> The body is not merely an object with which man is confronted, it is something which he himself IS.. The world too, is not just opposed to the body as the space outside it, it is rather its and our extension. Therefore, just as there is a distinction between the self and the body (i.e., man is not simply a body), so there is a unity we must affirm— man is really and truly corporeal in all his dimensions. It is only through this actual body quality that the spiritual nature comes to be.[9]

In his theology of the soul, Rahner has this to tell us:

> The doctrine of the soul, as an expression of man's self-understanding in general is part of the subject matter of general anthropology . . . Here it means the constitutive element by which human existence is capable, by nature, of attaining selfhood.[10]

As discussed earlier, Karl Rahner prefers the term "spirit" to the word "soul." Here he tells us:

> It is a fundamental concept in the history of philosophy. If the depth of the concept is to be grasped, it should not be constricted within the limits of a definition . . . The 'historicity' which is an essential property of the spirit, and the history which is its essential actuation, must be considered if we are to understand the concept.

Then, after several pages of his discussion on the historicity and the history above, Rahner concludes with the following statement concerning the spirit:

> Spirit as the self-realization of the immediacy of the presence of being also implies an essential relationship to the material cosmos. The spirit is the self-presentation of being as the unlimited whole . . . There can be therefore and there is nothing "outside" of the spirit . . . It follows then that the history of the spirit and the evolution of the cosmos do not draw further and further apart, but come constantly closer together.[11]

RAHNER ON DEATH AND
RESURRECTION OF THE BODY

In his theological primer, *Foundations of Christian Faith,* Rahner writes:

> The death of Jesus is such that by its very nature, it is subsumed into the resurrection. It is death into the resurrection. The resurrection is not a new period in the life of Jesus, it means rather and precisely the permanent, redeemed, final, and definitive validity of the single and unique life of Jesus.

In this theology, Rahner argues that the resurrection of Jesus and our own bodily resurrection is the central theme of the Christian faith and must be bestowed by God, for man's action itself is in every respect, acquiescence. Furthermore, without a body there is no real life. Our bodies insert us into the material world making us part of the universe and the universe part of us. As universal participants, we are also personally related to God.

The human person is simultaneously historical and transcendental and possesses reason ultimately as having the transcendental freedom to realize who they will become before God, i.e., who will be our final irrevocable self. Rahner conceptualized such freedom as the ability to make a fundamental option to either accept or reject the grace of God's self-communication. He further proposed that the soul after death retains a relationship to the materiality of the universe taken in its entirety.[12] He then states further:

Since the soul is united to the body, it clearly must also have some relationship to that whole of which the body is a part, that is, to the totality which constitutes the unity of the material universe. Further, if the soul, by its substantial union with the body as its essential form also has a relationship to this unity of the universe, it would then seem questionable that the separation of the body and soul in an earthly death should involve the definite cessation of the soul's relation to the universe.

Thus, the relationship of the soul to the universe implies that the soul, by surrendering its limited and worldly bodily structure at death, then becomes open towards the universe. In this way the new and glorified body would become the perfect expression of the eternal relationship of the glorified person to the universe as a whole.[13]

Man is always present to himself in his entirety. He can place everything in question. In his book, *Hearers of the Word*, Rahner further affirms not only the reality of transcendence, but also the reality of God, who as "Holy Mystery," always exceeds being fully grasped by humanity. Man shows himself to be a being with an infinite horizon. The human person is transcendence, always moving beyond the self to the ever-greater God. However, as you get closer to any horizon, another horizon opens up. So, death is one's definitive and final act of transcendental freedom whereby one determines one's eternal destiny. Such self-determination takes place throughout one's life, in and through one's categorical choices, but in dying, such a process is brought to a final and definitive end. However, soul and body cannot be separated at death. On the other hand, the resurrected body would be an evolved spiritual body. [14]

Resurrection should not be viewed as a return to life and existence in time and space as we experience it. Therefore, the human person seeks a definitive realization of freedom, and this realization must be bodily since the human person is unified as spirit-in-matter. The person would reach the fullness of perfection only at the end of the world in a bodily resurrection whereby soul and glorified body would thus be united. However, Rahner asserts that Jesus has already achieved the fullness of resurrected life. The resurrection of Jesus validates his claim to have brought the Kingdom of God into the world and that the Kingdom is in our midst. Only after the resurrection did others come to fully realize Jesus's true identity as the Son of God. The death and resurrection of Jesus is God's final Word spoken into the silence of the universe and the unsurpassable self-communication of God. In his theological primer, *Foundations of Christian Faith*, Rahner maintains that:

The resurrection (of Jesus) speaks to us immediately because of its character as an answer to the question about the meaning of everything . . . It calls us in an essentially radical way, more than the individual miracles in the life of Jesus.[15]

Jesus was the "firstborn" from the dead (Col. 1:18, Acts 3:15, 1 Cor. 15:20–28) and the consummation of the world has already begun. It is Jesus Christ who has already ushered in the beginning of the "end of the world." Rahner's view was that we must fit what we call the "Resurrection of the Body" into the context of the history of the universe which will one day come to an end.[16]

Revelation should not be seen as information about God, but as God's own self-disclosure to us. The resurrection of Jesus is the absolute self-communication of God. Human persons actualize their transcendental freedom, including knowing God, through concrete acts of loving God and neighbor. Rahner maintained that the human person is capable of two things—"loving" and "knowing," with a primacy for loving. In its truest and most complete sense, all knowing is fulfilled in loving; knowledge must be guided by love. What makes the human person different is that we are the only creature that knows that we know. Rahner grounded the human quest for knowledge in God who is the source of all grace-given knowledge. Similarly, the human quest for real love is grounded in an intrinsic, even if unconscious, need for the source of all love who is God, the Absolute and Holy Mystery. All human love originates in God and is grace-given. History is dynamic and not static, thus the only thing permanent in all of the history of the universe from beginning to end is and will continue to be "love."

Rahner states that the death and the resurrection of Jesus are two aspects of a single event not to be separated. Even though the resurrection is not a historical event in time and place, like the death and crucifixion of Jesus, it can be seen as "transhistorical." The resurrection event affects the entire history of the universe, takes place on the other side of death, and lies beyond the boundaries of time and space. It is an event in history which has consequences for everyone for all time. This puts the resurrection beyond the reach of all history and historians. This event cannot be envisioned as a return to life in the temporal sphere, but the seal of approval of God the Father upon all that Jesus stood for prior to his resurrection. Any approach to Rahner's theology must take into consideration his theology of grace. For him, God's grace is the ground of human identity. Grace is what sustains the human being, and God's grace is what guides the human person towards God-self through the grace of God's self-communication. God is the principle and the ground of the human person, and only in such a horizon can the human being become truly a person. Through his cross and resurrection as a single event, Jesus became our savior. Jesus Christ as the "God as human" has enabled God the Father to establish his grace-filled saving will in the world historically, universally, personally, and unequivocally. God loves us unconditionally, but we did nothing to earn God's love, for He has already given that love to us gratuitously and irrevocably. Rahner claims that love is the key to understanding the meaning of human freedom. God is love and we are fully human to the extent that we as humans love. Love is the fundamental act that embraces every aspect of human life and is the only constant in the universe from beginning to end. We as human persons are given the freedom to love both God and neighbor and to either accept or reject this God-given grace to love as well as to choose who will be our final irrevocable self. [17]

RESURRECTION AND HUMAN EXPERIENCE

As discussed previously, to Rahner, the term 'Body' implies that it is the whole man in his proper embodied reality. 'Resurrection' then means, therefore, the termination and perfection of the whole man before God, which gives him 'eternal life.' In terms of resurrection and human experience, Rahner will tell us that "the whole is more than the sum of its parts." Also, that resurrection is certainly not an occurrence which we can understand on the basis of our own experience. Furthermore, only those who hope can see the fulfillment of hope, and at the sight of its fulfilment, hope attains the purpose of its existence. This "circle" neither needs to be, nor can be broken—but men called to hope for the resurrection of their own flesh (which they are, and do not simply possess) can by God's grace "spring into that circle." So, the experienced reality of the risen Christ "provides the ground of the experience" and conversely the event "manifests" itself only to faith.

We do not need to imagine what someone in the genuine totality of his human existence looks like "with body and soul." We can calmly admit that we cannot imagine a spiritized-bodily resurrection because unlike, for example, the raising of dead to life, it is not and is not intended to be "the restoration of a previous state" but a "transformation of a radical kind." In the New Testament, there are reports of the resurrection of the son of the widow at Nain, the daughter of Jairus, and of course, Lazarus. However, the resurrection of Jesus is not at all similar. Unlike those examples, Jesus will not die again. What this tells us is that in the future, "Resurrection of the Body"—the "whole man" is brought to perfect fulfilment. We cannot divide this whole man into an ever-valid "spirit" and a merely provisional "body." The resurrected person is the glorified and inseparable body and soul. In his theology, Rahner noted that "since the soul is united to the body, it clearly must also have some relationship to that whole of which the body is a part, that is, to the totality which constitutes the unity of the material universe." The personal identity of each human being would be forever linked with our universe—even after the Resurrection of the Body. However, the resurrected body would be an evolved spiritized and glorified body.[18]

THE RISEN CHRIST IS THE UNIVERSAL CHRIST

Toward the end of Karl Rahner's life, he pointed to the need for a systematic theology that brings together the relationship between the risen Jesus Christ and the transformation of the universe through systematizing a theology combined with the natural sciences. This would require research which would bring together elements of the meaning of creation, self-transcendence, and the self-communication of God as grace. This would entail seeing the risen Christ as the Universal Christ and the beginning of the transformation of the universe, the hope of seeing God as the absolute future of the universe, and further developing Rahner's Transcendental Anthropology. Rahner devoted considerable emphasis on writing about this dialogue between science and theology in his later essays. He particularly highlights and identifies a need to further develop the thought of French paleontologist and Jesuit theologian, Pierre Teilhard de Chardin. This would show the connection between Jesus of Nazareth as the risen and Universal Christ and his being the Omega point of world evolution. More will be said on this later in chapter 17 of this book which is titled, "The Risen Christ iIs the Universal Christ.." [19]

NOTES

1. "Your Show of Shows," Sid Caesar, *Encyclopedia.com,* https://www.encyclopedia.com/people/literature-and-arts/film-and-television-biographies/sid-caesar.
2. Karl Rahner, *Encyclopedia of Theology, Sacramentum Mundi* (New York, NY: Seabury Press, 1975)/ Karl Rahner, *Foundations of Christian Faith: An Introduction to the Idea of Christianity* (New York, NY: Crossroads, 1995).
3. St Anselm, *Catholicism*, Richard McBrien (Harper Collins, San Fran., CA,1994 p. 20).
4. Karl Rahner, *Encyclopedia of Theology, Sacramentum Mundi.* (New York, NY: Seabury Press, 1975, p. 880).
5. Ibid. Ch. 13, f.2 (FCF, see pp. 116–195)(SM see pp. 1734–1736).
6. K. Rahner, "Anonymous Christians," *Theological Investigations* 6 (London, Eng.: Darton, Longman & Todd, 1982), pp. 390–398).
7. Ibid. Ch. 13, f. 2, (FCF p. 126).
8. K. Rahner, "Natural Science and Reasonable Faith: Theological Perspectives for Dialogue with the Natural Sciences," in *Theological Investigations* 21, trans. Hugh M. Riley (NY: Crossroad, 1988 pp. 1–44, (See also K. Rahner, *Foundations of Christian Faith: An Introduction to the Idea of Christianity* (New York, NY: Crossroads, 1995, pp. 1–34; 268–437).
9. Ibid. Ch.13, f. 4 pp. 157–158.
10. Ibid. Ch. 13. f. 4 p. 165.
11. Ibid. Ch. 13 f. 4, pp. 1619–1623.

12. Ibid. Ch. 13 f. 2 (FCF, p. 266).

13. Karl Rahner, *The Theology of Death* (New York, NY: Herder and Herder, 1961, p.1–65).

14. Ibid. Ch. 13 f. 4, pp. 1430–1453, 1734–1736, Ibid. Ch. 13. F. 2, FCF p. 31 see also K. Rahner, *Hearers of the Word* (New York, NY: Herder & Herder, 1969).

15. Ibid Ch. 13. f..2 (FCF p. 264).

16. Karl Rahner, "Resurrection of the Body," (*Theological Investigations* 2, pp. 212–213).

17. K. Rahner, "Nature and Grace," *Theological Investigations* 4 pp. 165–188. See also K. Rahner, *Foundations of Christian Faith: An Introduction to the Idea of Christianity,* (New York, NY: Crossroads, 1995, pp. 1–311).

18. Karl Rahner, "Resurrection of the Body," (*Theological Investigations* 2, pp. 210–211). See also K. Rahner, *On the Theology of Death* (C.H. Henkey; Quaestiones disputatae Vol. 2; (New York, Herder and Herder, 1961). See also K. Rahner, *Foundations of Christian Faith, An Introduction to the Idea of Christianity* (New York, NY: Crossroads, 1995, pp. 178–264).

19. Karl Rahner, *Theological Investigations and Essays* volume 21:227. See also De Chardin, Pierre Teilhard, *Phenomenon of Man* (New York, NY: Harper Collins, 1975, pp. 257–298). See also chapter 17 of this book, "The Risen Christ Is the Universal Christ."

Chapter 12

Signs in the Natural World

Dying and Rising

If there is one fundamental truth about the human condition, it is the inevitable reality of earthly death, but because the natural world often reflects spiritual truth, resurrection can be pictured throughout nature. It was St. Augustine, followed by St. Thomas Aquinas in his *Summa* who said, "grace follows nature" or "grace builds on nature."[1] We might extend this theological understanding to say as well, "extraordinary follows ordinary" or even "rising follows dying." That is assuming, of course, that we see dying as something not only inevitable, but as "graced nature." This could imply further that everything in nature is significant, no matter how seemingly insignificant or small. Therefore, we should not ignore or minimize what ordinary natural things can show us sacramentally.

Taking the word "sacrament" in its broadest sense, as a visible sign of something invisible or sacred and hidden, we could say that the whole natural world is a vast sacramental system in that many material things are unto humankind, the signs of things spiritual and sacred. The presence of God can often be revealed in many natural and visible realities, but God will always remain more than that. Anything else is not God, but merely an idol. Many things in nature are imbued with the hidden presence of God. Therefore, they can be a sign of grace or a natural signal of transcendence. If all of nature can be imbued with the mysterious and hidden presence of God, this would necessarily imply that God can choose to become present to us and reveal Godself to us through nature in other people, events, animals, objects, the earth and universe around us, or for that matter, anything natural, material, tangible, visible, or as an event occurring in history. This would include death and resurrection.

Because of the principle of sacramentality, all of nature can have a hidden character. The Holy Mystery that is God can be seen in virtually everyone and everything around us. St. Francis of Assisi is a good example of someone who experienced this. St. Francis saw God mysteriously reflected in the sun, moon, and stars. He saw God in animals as well as everyone and everything around him. If all that is visible and material in the natural world around us can convey the mystery of a hidden God, then that should say to us that all reality has a sacramental and mysterious character. It is essentially "graced nature." That should further imply that all visible or natural reality can be mediated to us by the unveiling of its meaning to us by the Holy Spirit. The death and resurrection of Jesus Christ should be no exception to what the natural world around us can point to and reveal to us.[2]

When we observe nature, we see a continuous transformation and development from a simple and often hidden program to a more intricate, developed, complex, and "glorious" one. For example, a flower from a tiny seedling or a fully grown tree emerging from the program lying within its respective seed is a mystery, in that unless a seed dies, it cannot produce life. When the shell of the seed becomes soft in the ground and is nourished with water and warmed by the sun, it somehow germinates, puts forth roots, and then transforms as it sprouts out of the earth. After that, it grows and produces fruit and many more seeds. Closer to home, a fully developed muti-trillion celled human person emerges from a fertilized egg and embryo. Would it then be a stretch to envision a glorified body emerging from a dead one? Furthermore, isn't it magnificent to just imagine that even our Lord and Savior, Jesus Christ, the King of Glory, was once a tiny fetus whose entire universe was the womb of his Mother, Mary? He was comforted in hearing her heartbeat and being nourished only by an attachment to her umbilical cord. As radically different as the world will be from the womb for all newborns including Jesus, so will death and resurrected life be from life in the world. The life and death and resurrection cycle will continue as grace will always and eternally follow nature and build on nature.

In the Gospels, even Jesus uses natural means to describe the concept of resurrection. In the Gospel of John for instance, Jesus will give the disciples this example from the natural world as a foreshadowing of his own death and resurrection:

> Amen, amen, I say to you, unless a grain of wheat falls to the ground and dies, it remains just a grain of wheat; but if it dies, it produces much fruit. (Jn. 12:24)

All the disciples would be able to comprehend at that time was the natural sense that Jesus was using as an example from agriculture of how a seed dies and is buried in the ground and then it bears fruit. This had been the case for all to see as far back as people could remember. The disciples just couldn't wrap their heads around how that related to Jesus's imminent crucifixion, death, and resurrection. Soon they would see for themselves and be able to grasp exactly what Jesus had been talking about.

The Apostle Paul also draws some comparisons between the tiny seed, its dying, and a glorious bodily resurrection in his first Letter to the Corinthians:

> But someone may say, "How are the dead raised? With what kind of body will they come back?" You fool! What you sow is not brought to life unless it dies. And what you sow is not the body that is to be but a bare kernel of wheat, perhaps, or of some other kind; but God gives it a body as he chooses, and to each of the seeds its own body. Not all flesh is the same, but there is one kind for human beings, another kind of flesh for animals, another kind of flesh for birds, and another for fish. There are both heavenly bodies and earthly bodies, but the brightness of the heavenly is one kind and that of the earthly another. The brightness of the sun is one kind, the brightness of the moon another, and the brightness of the stars another. For star differs from star in brightness. So also, is the resurrection of the dead. It is sown corruptible; it is raised incorruptible. It is sown dishonorable; it is raised glorious. It is sown weak; it is raised powerful. It is sown a natural body; it is raised a spiritual body. If there is a natural body, there is also a spiritual one. (1 Cor. 15:35–44)[3]

If we look at the natural world around us more closely, we will also see many more examples of dying and rising. The sun rises each morning to bring light, as the new day follows night, and this cycle has been occurring since time began. In looking at the seasons, spring and summer always follow the dead of winter. Leaves on trees turn brown and die off in the fall and winter and then as tiny buds appear, it turns them a vibrant green in spring, while in the summer much fruit is borne. Following that, in the fall, the dying process begins all over again. In nature, the cycle of rising unto new life continually follows after the process of death and dying.

There are many animals that are symbolic of dying and rising as well. The dove is a symbol of resurrected life in the Holy Spirit. The dove appeared at Jesus's baptism on earth where it descended from Heaven and rested upon Him (Jn. 1:32). It is one of the few symbols that has retained both its natural appearance and its deeper spiritual significance from the beginning of Christianity to the present day. The eagle is also symbolic of resurrection and of renewal (Is. 40:31). The eagle flies high into the sky towards the sun. It is a symbol of St. John referring to the prophecy in Ezekiel 1:5,10 dealing with the four living creatures. The resurrected Christ can be likened to an eagle soaring high into the sky after aspiring to seek the truths of God to bring God's Kingdom into our midst here on earth.

Jesus often told those who sought a sign from him that "No sign will be given except the sign of Jonah (Mt. 12:38–42)." In the Bible, Jonah is thrown off a boat by sailors to calm down the stormy sea. Jonah is swallowed by a whale and stays in the animal's body for three days and three nights. Then the animal spits him out, and he ends up on the beach. The natural symbol of the whale symbolizes a transition between life and death and between death and resurrection. The belly of the whale is simultaneously a realm of death and rebirth. This episode is an allegory for Jesus's dying and rising as the whale is, at one and the same time, the place where both impending death and then resurrection takes place.

The lamb is often considered to be our Angus Dei, "The Lamb of God," and is most frequently used to represent Jesus Christ (Jn. 1:29). In a natural sense, the lamb is slain but its sign of resurrected life is portrayed many ways—with a halo; with a victory wreath, carrying a banner of victory, wearing a crown, seated on a book with seven seals, or standing on a hill with four streams of water flowing from it, representing the four Gospels. Finally, in the poetic and majestic imagery of the Book of Revelation, this victorious Lamb who was slain is resurrected and stands in the midst of the throne of God (Rev. 5:6, 7:17, 22:3). There are so many more animals such as the lion which is another natural symbol of the king, and the symbolism for the resurrected Savior's role as "The Lion of Judah," and the King of Kings (Rev. 17:14, 19). There is also the fish (Ichtus), whose letters in Greek are an acronym for symbolizing the words "Jesus Christ, Son of God and Savior." There are countless other animals who are natural symbols for the resurrected Jesus but even mentioning those could fill another entire book.

In the insect world, we see the lifecycle of the creeping earthbound caterpillar as it willingly encases itself in its own self-made tomb and completely dissolves, becoming a chrysalis. From this inglorious tomb emerges the beautifully new and more glorious body of the emergent butterfly. The rebirth of this new creation is capable of higher movements and increased possibilities which were impossible in its earthbound original state of being. Life goes on in a new and transformed state. The universe around us can give us so many examples of how God the Father uses the world of "Mother Nature" to point the way to the resurrected Christ and allows us to then envision the possibility of our own future bodily resurrection.[4]

THE WOOD OF THE CROSS AND THE TREE OF LIFE

A wooden cross can be a natural symbol that Jesus has risen from the grave and been resurrected as well as signifying a believer's commitment to Jesus Christ and the Christian faith. It is also a natural symbol of our own future bodily resurrection from the dead. In contrast, a crucifix symbolizes Jesus's suffering and death on the cross. When Christ rose from the grave, he defeated sin and death. Therefore, the empty wooden cross is not only a symbol of Jesus resurrection from the dead, but also a sign of the glorious victory won by Jesus Christ by demonstrating for all eternity, his love for us. The victory Christ won through the wood of his cross and resurrection and its symbolic connection to the tree of life is reaffirmed in reading the Book of Revelation Ch. 2:7; 5:12; 17:14; 19:16; 22:2, 14, 19.

A tree has historically been a natural symbol of life or "living wood." The tree of life, however, represents resurrected life and the connection between earth and heaven. The fact that the tree of life in the Biblical book of Genesis is in the middle of the mythical Garden of Eden in Paradise is significant (Gn. 2:9). It can be seen as a prefiguration of the cross and resurrection of Christ. Furthermore, it implies that the life it offers is not inherent to the tree but is a divine gift of God's grace that comes through the tree. The tree of life imparts God's own eternal life as well as demonstrates to us his constant living and loving presence in our midst.[5]

WATER

Water is a key natural resource which is essential for all life on earth. In fact, even the bodies of human beings are made up of 60% water and 55% of our blood is plasma which is 90% water. Since life on earth began, water has been a natural symbol of cleansing, purifying, rebirth, and renewal. Some of the unique characteristics of water are that it has the ability to cleanse itself of discoloring and dirt and become pure and clean once again. In addition to human beings cleansing themselves physically, water is also seen as a means of spiritual rebirth and renewal. Additionally, it is a natural sign of dying and rising to new life in many World Religions, including Christianity. Water is used in many baptismal rituals. In the Scriptures, water is one of the natural symbols for the Holy Spirit. Many people bathe in holy rivers, believing that they have washed away their sins and are reborn again. In countless religious creation accounts, water is seen as the source of life itself as well as a sign of rebirth and a giver of new life. It can be a natural sign and symbol for creation, destruction, purification, rebirth, and love. Christ, as the source of "living water," walked on water, and changed water into wine, thus these acts alone can be seen as a transcendence of the natural condition represented by water or as "graced nature.."

Water has historically been seen to be a natural sign of the divine. In China, 600 years before Christ was born, a poet-philosopher by the name of Lao-Tse, the author of the *Tao*, wrote these words concerning water:

> The supreme good is like water, which is the source of nourishment to almost all the living creatures on earth. It gives life to thousands of things without striving

and competing . . . It is content with the low places that people disdain . . . One cannot reflect in streaming water. Only those who know internal peace can give it to others . . . Have patience. Be still and allow the mud to settle and wait until the water is clear . . . Water will wear away rock, which is rigid and cannot yield. As a rule, whatever is fluid, soft, and yielding will overcome whatever is rigid and hard. This is another paradox: what is soft is strong . . . the river and the sea are sovereign over the valleys because they take the "lower position." Water is the perfect embodiment of the *Tao* because, by being submissive and flowing wherever it can go, water is powerful . . . All streams flow to the sea because it is lower than they are. Humility gives it its power."[6]

After reading the words of Lao-Tse in the *Tao*, it would be virtually impossible not to see water as "graced nature" or a symbol of the divine. As a natural symbol of purity, cleansing, rebirth, and renewal, the presence of water in the natural world can reveal much to us spiritually about the resurrected Jesus Christ, the fountain of life, who gives us "living water" because he is the living God.

NOTES

1. "Grace" New Advent Catholic Encyclopedia, K. Knight, ed. T. Aquinas, *Summa Theolologica*, Question 110, found online 1/2/23, https://www.newadvent.org/summa /2110.htm; see also Question 2, https://www.newadvent.org/summa/1002.htm.

2. "Sacrament/Sacramentality" M. Hickey, *Get Real,* (Lanham, Md., University Press, 2012, Ch. 11); see also R. McBrien, *Catholicism* (New York, NY, Harper Collins Pub., 1994, pp. 782–800).

3. Ibid. Ch. 1 f. 3.

4. https://www.christiansymbols.net/animals.html see also https://buildfaith .org/jesus-and-the-symbol-of-animals/. https://www.encyclopedia.com/religion/ encyclopedias-almanacs-transcripts-and-maps/animals-symbolism. MLA citation. Cret, Paul. "Animals in Christian Art." The Catholic Encyclopedia. Vol. 1. New York: Robert Appleton Company, 1907. 15 Dec. 2022, http://www.newadvent .org/cathen/01515b.htm. Also https://www.newadvent.org/cathen/01221a.htmhttps:// www.newadvent.org/cathen/01220a.htmhttps://www.newadvent.org/cathen/08755b .htmhttps://symbolsage.com/symbols-of-rebirth-and-their-meanings/ https://www .encyclopedia.com/religion/encyclopedias-almanacs-transcripts-and-maps/lamb-god.

5. https://www.newadvent.org/cathen/14519a.htm. See also T. Aquinas, Summa, Q. 97, Art IV, found online at https://www.newadvent.org/summa/1097.htm#article4.

6. Lao-Tse, *The Tao-Te Ching*, The M.I.T. Classics Archive, online edition, http:// classics.mit.edu/Lao/taote.html.

Chapter 13

Symbols in Mythology
Dying and Rising

The concept of death and resurrection predates the Christian religion by several centuries. A dying-and-rising, death-rebirth, or resurrected deity is a religious motif in which a god or goddess dies and returns to life. Examples of gods who die and later return to life are most often cited from the religions of the ancient Near East, and traditions influenced by them include Greco-Roman mythology in which most of us have a greater familiarity. In much of mythology, the cycle of death and resurrection is often parodied. World mythology is full of religious figures who have undergone death, been transformed, and then a returned to life. The purpose of showing them here in this chapter is intended to mention them strictly as a metaphor to Christian faith and belief in the dying and rising of Jesus Christ. Here are just a few.

ADONIS

Adonis, for example, is known to be the Greek god of resurrection and rebirth. In addition, the myth involves his everlasting mistress Astarte, the goddess of love and beauty. She was known as Aphrodite in the Greek myths and as Venus to the Romans. Adonis is said to be the god of many things, such as fertility, vegetation, beauty, and desire, but he is best known for being the Greek god of rebirth. The central idea of the myth is that the death and resurrection of Adonis, represents the decay of nature every fall and winter and its revival and renewal in the spring and summer.[1]

OSIRIS

In ancient Egypt, Osiris was the god of resurrection. There are several versions of the myth of Osiris, but most all of them tell of his death and rebirth. On one occasion, jealous rivals murdered Osiris and cast him into the Nile River. His sister-wife, Isis, found the body and returned him to life with the help of a magic spell, but Osiris soon died once again. This time his body was ripped to pieces and scattered across the world. Isis gathered up the fragments and joined them together for a decent burial. When the other gods saw the extent of Isis' devotion, they rewarded Osiris by resurrecting him and making him the god of the dead who returns to a new life.

TAMMUZ

The myth of Tammuz and Ishtar shows considerable similarity to the myth of Osiris and Isis. Tammuz was killed every year by a wild boar but was rescued from the nether world by Ishtar, who brought him back to life and assured a new springtime. The natural cycle of dying and a return to new life was thus symbolized in this dying-and-rising myth as well.[2]

DIONYSUS

Dionysus was also referred to as BACCHUS, a Roman deity. He was the Greek god of vegetation, fertility, the grape harvest, fruit, and wine. He was also associated with weddings, death, sacrifice, and sexuality. He was said to have been the offspring of Zeus and Demeter and the brother of Apollo, Artemis, Athena, and Persephone among others. In Greek mythology, Dionysus was a horned child who was torn to pieces by Titans who then boiled and ate him. Zeus then destroyed the Titans by thunderbolts because of their actions against Dionysus; then from the ashes, humans were formed. Following this, however, Dionysus's grandmother Rhea managed to put some of his pieces back together beginning with his heart that was spared. She brought him back to life. Some scholars have suggested that because of this myth, Dionysus became an example of death and resurrection in mythology. A common theme in early depictions was the metamorphosis of Dionysus at the hands of the gods, transforming his frenzied followers into hybrid creatures, usually represented by both tame and wild satyrs. This was also seen to represent a dying and rising in the transition from a civilized social life and a returning back to the wildness of nature as a means of escape. Dionysus was also the god of myth and theater. Wine was naturally a religious focus in the cult of Dionysus/Bacchus and was his earthly incarnation. Festivals of Dionysus included the performance of sacred dramas as he was seen to be the initial driving force behind the development of theatre in Western culture. The religious cult of Dionysus saw him as a divine communicant between the living and the dead. For this additional reason, he is also sometimes categorized as a dying-and-rising god.[3]

ODIN

In Norse mythology the chief God was Odin, who gained great wisdom by undergoing several trials. To achieve mysterious knowledge from beyond the realm of the dead, Odin decided to sacrifice himself. It was said that he took a spear and drove it into his side. Then he tied a noose to the world-tree and hung himself for nine days. It was after this sacrifice that Odin returned to life stronger than ever before. If this tale of death and resurrection sounds vaguely familiar, it is probably because Christianity had reached northern Europe long before the writing of the Poems dedicated to Odin and would have coexisted in the north country alongside the Norse religion.[4]

ATTIS

Attis was a Phrygian god who was worshipped in Asia Minor and later entered the Greek and Roman pantheons as the partner of the goddess Cybele. He was born from an almond nurtured in the body of a goddess. Attis was just about to be married to a princess when the goddess Cybele showed up, throwing Attis into a frenzy. Having gone mad, he then mutilated himself and bled to death. Cybele relented and brought Attis back to life, resurrected in the form of a pine tree. Attis was a vegetarian god who, in his self-mutilation, death, and resurrection, represents the seeds and fruits of the earth, which must die in winter only to rise again to new life in the spring.[5]

DEMETER AND PERSEPHONE

Demeter was the Greek goddess of agriculture who sustained mankind with the earth's rich bounty. Additionally, she was the goddess of the cycle of life, death, and rebirth. She presided over the foremost of the Mystery Cults which promised its initiates the path to a blessed rebirth in the afterlife in the realm of Elysium. In Ovid's *Metamorphoses* we find the myth of Zeus, the king of the gods, and Demeter whose daughter, Persephone, falls in love with the brother of Zeus, Hades, the lord of death and the underworld. Demeter would have none of this marriage and demanded that Zeus return Persephone to her mother. Hades was afraid of losing her and allowed Persephone to spend half the year with her mother, Demeter, on Mt Olympus and the other half of the year with Hades in the underworld. The central idea of this myth was an explanation of how the seasons of the year came to be. During the time that Persephone spends away from her mother, Demeter causes the earth to wither and die. This time of year eventually was seen as autumn and winter and signaled a time of death and dying. When Persephone comes back to her mother for the other half of the year in spring and summer, Persephone's arrival signals a renewal of hope and abundance as the earth becomes fertile and fruitful, experiencing renewed life. It is seen to complete the cycle from death and dying as it becomes a time of renewal, rebirth, and resurrection. The Sumerian myth of the goddess, Inanna, shows many similarities to this one while again emphasizing the theme of death, rebirth, and resurrection.[6]

THE PHOENIX

The Phoenix was a mythical bird of great beauty which was said to have first lived in the Arabian wilderness. Its life span was seen to be between three hundred and five hundred years. Periodically, it burned itself upon a funeral pyre; whereupon it would rise from its own ashes, resurrected and restored to all the vigor of youth. Hence, it would enter upon a new cycle of life. Rebirth through fire was the only mode of resurrection for this mythical bird.

The Phoenix was introduced into Christian symbolism as early as the first century, when the legend of this bird was related by St. Clement in his first Epistle to the Corinthians and by Tertullian *(De Resurrection 13)* and Origen *(Contra Celsum 4.98)*, as well as other of the Church Fathers. In early Catholic art, the Phoenix constantly appears on funeral stones, with its particular meaning being the resurrection of the dead and the triumph of eternal life over death. The Phoenix later became a symbol commonly connected with the crucifixion and resurrection of Jesus Christ. The Phoenix is certainly a good metaphor for the death and resurrection of Christ, but we should not fail to remember that it is, Mythology, after all, while the crucifixion, death, and resurrection of Christ is something not strictly mythological but moreover, grounded in holy mystery as the home of reality.[7]

THE OUROBOROS

The Ouroboros was a mythical serpent of ancient Egypt and Greece. It is most often represented in a circular fashion with its tail in its mouth, continually devouring itself and thus being reborn from itself. The Ouroboros depicts the unity of all things, particularly those material and spiritual, which never disappear but perpetually change form in an eternal cycle of destruction, dying, and rebirth. There is a school of thought which believes that the yin-yang symbol which originated in China, depicting a unity of opposites, such as earth and heaven, male and female, matter and spirit, light and dark etc. evolved and transformed to eventually become the symbol of the Ouroboros in Greek mythology. There are also different depictions of the Ouroboros which are shown to be in the form of the infinity symbol representing the recreation of life through death within the universe.[8]

THE UNICORN

The Unicorn is a mythological horse-like creature with a horn and wings. Like the Phoenix (the legendary bird that dies and rises from its ashes), the Unicorn was adopted by Christians as a symbol of Christ. In Christian thought, the Unicorn, though mythological, represents the incarnation of Christ. It was a symbol of purity, majesty, rarity, and grace that could be captured only by a virgin. Folklore says that it had a single tricolored, eighteen-inch-long horn between its eyes, a white body with wings, a purple head, and dark blue eyes. If captured by a virgin, the Unicorn would obligingly fall asleep in her lap although, the virgin-unicorn relationship appears to pre-date any Christian influence.

In the Bible, the word "horn" has many different meanings. On the one hand, it signified terror and defeat toward enemies by animals endowed with a horn (see Dn. 8:1–27), but it further signified victory, magnificence, strength, dominion, honor, dignity, nobility, great power, and glory. In the Old Testament, this was sometimes applied to Yahweh and his anointed (see Ps. 18:3; 1 Sam. 2:10). In the New Testament, the Gospel writer Luke will apply this metaphorically to Christ in Chapter One in a verse which follows after the Canticle of Mary:

> Blessed be the Lord, the God of Israel, for he has visited and brought redemption to his people. He has raised up a horn for our salvation within the house of David his servant. (Lk. 1:68–69)

A famous series of tapestries, now housed in The New York Metropolitan Museum "The Cloisters," depicts a Unicorn in seven scenes. The tapestries are also called the "Hunt of the Unicorn" and have strong ties to the Paschal Mystery of Christ. The first tapestry shows the Unicorn healing the waters of a stream by touching it with its horn. In the various other scenes, the Unicorn is captured, killed and then is resurrected and shown alive again in the last tapestry.

When Greeks attempted to translate the Hebrew Bible, the word *re'em* caused many problem issues for the translators as they had no equivalent word. They, therefore, substituted their best word, *monokeros,* which meant "one-horned," and this led to subsequent issues with the translations until we ultimately ended up with the word "Unicorn" as the best equivalent. Subsequently, many of the early church Fathers drew parallels to the incarnation of Christ and wrote allegories about the Unicorn representing the incarnation of Christ. These included Tertullian, Justin Martyr, St. Basil, and St. Ambrose to name a few. In fact, in his commentary on the Psalms, St Ambrose had this to say concerning the allegory of the Unicorn and the death and resurrection of Jesus Christ:

Who then is this Unicorn, but the only-begotten Son of God?[9]

On a trip to Northern Italy a few years ago, my wife Terri and I took a tour boat and visited the castle of St. Charles Borromeo, which sits in the middle of Lake Maggiore. The former Bishop of Milan, St. Charles Borromeo, died in 1584 and the Borromeo family still maintains the castle along with many of his sculptures and artworks. There we saw hanging, many of his beautiful, multi-colored, and intricately woven tapestries replete with countless Unicorns, all in many various scenes signifying the incarnation, death, and resurrection of Jesus Christ. Seeing those Unicorn tapestries was one of the most memorable highlights of our trip and caused me to begin to reflect further on the allegory of the Unicorn and its intimate relatedness to the Incarnation, death, and Resurrection of Jesus Christ.[10]

NOTES

1. https://www.worldhistory.org/Adonis/; see also https://www.*britannica.com/*topic/Adonis-Greek-mythology. https://study.com/academy/lesson/who-is-adonis-in-greek-mythology-story-facts.html

2. https://www.*britannica.com/*topic/Osiris-Egyptian-god. https://theculturetrip.com/europe/united-kingdom/articles/rebirth-and-resurrection-spring-myths-of-the-ancient-world/

3. http://www.biblicalcatholic.com/apologetics/JesusEvidenceCrucifiedSaviors .htm#Dionysos

4. https://www.*britannica.com*/topic/Odin-Norse-deity

5.https://www.*britannica.com*/topic/Attishttps://www.theoi.com/Phrygios/Attis .html; https://www.greekmytholgy.com/Myths/Mortals/Attis/attis.html; https:// greekgodsandgoddesses.net/gods/attis/; https://www.ancient-origins.net/myths -legends-europe/pagan-attis-and-christian-jesus-spurious-connection-009634; https: //mythologysource.com/who-was-attis-greek-myth/; https://www.jstor.org/stable /4433594; http://www.*mythencyclopedia*.com/Ar-Be/Attis.html

6. https://www.*britannica.com*/topic/Demeter; https://www.theoi.com/articles/ what-is-the-demeter-and-persephone-story-summarized/Ovid, *Metamorphoses* 5. 354 ff (trans. Melville) (Roman epic C1st BC to C1st AD). https://canvas.uw.edu/courses /862997/pages/demeter-and-persephone; https://www.greekmyths-greekmythology .com/myth-of-hades-and-persephone/; https://www.greeka.com/greece-myths/ persephone/

7. https://interestingliterature.com/2021/04/phoenix-symbolism-in-literature-and -myth/; https://www.vision.org/mythical-phoenix-in-early-church-writings-225; https://www.newworldencyclopedia.org/entry/phoenix_(mythology)

8. https://www.britannica.com/topic/Ouroboroshttps://mythologian.net/ouroboros -symbol-of-infinity/

9. St. Ambrose, *Patrologia Latina*; see also online https://www.sacred-texts.com/ etc/lou/lou05.htm.

10. https://www.thecompassnews.org/2019/03/the-unicorn-at-the -annunciation/ (see also, *The Catholic Encyclopedia; A Handbook of Symbols in Christian Art*); https://unicornyard.com/unicorns-in-the-bible/ https://biblicalhorizons.com/open-book/no-28-concerning-unicorns/

Chapter 14

The Shroud of Turin

The Shroud of Turin is a piece of rectangular linen cloth measuring 14 ft 5 in × 3 ft 7 in. and bearing the negative image of a scourged and crucified man approximately six foot tall. It was discovered in the year 1354 and has been kept in the chapel of the Cathedral of Turin, in Northern Italy since the year 1578. When the first widely circulated photograph of the Shroud revealed the phenomenal image on it in 1898, it triggered an interest that has not since abated. New Testament accounts of Christ's Crucifixion in all four canonical Gospels had mentioned a linen cloth in which His body was wrapped (See Mk. 15:42–47; Mt. 27:57–61; Lk. 23:50–56; Jn. 19:38–42). Some describe the image on the Shroud as depicting Jesus of Nazareth and believe the fabric is the actual burial shroud in which Jesus was wrapped after his crucifixion and prior to his resurrection. Many believers consider it a sacred relic and a Christian icon. This remains an open question. The next biggest question, concerning the Shroud, however, seems to be how the image on the Shroud was made and if it can provide us with any relevant evidence of the resurrection.[1]

In 1978, a team of scientific researchers with the acronym "STURP" (Shroud of Turin Research Project) was allowed for the first time to carry out the most in-depth scientific comprehensive study of the Turin Shroud ever conducted. After spending 120 hours with much visual examination, and after taking thousands of photographs, countless macro and micro photographic studies, a considerable number of X-Ray radiographies; Infra-Red, visible and Ultra-Violet reflectance spectroscopies, as well as comprehensive fluorescence studies, the following is what they found: The answer to the question of how the image was produced on the linen or what produced the image remains as it has in the past, a complete and total mystery. At this time, science and technology cannot provide a satisfactory answer to that important question. In 1980, two years after the Shroud of Turin Research Project conducted their exhaustive testing, National Geographic magazine published a landmark article on the Shroud, utilizing the STURP photography. It was the article which ran in National Geographic that propelled the Shroud of Turin into the science and mainstream limelight after calling the Shroud, "One of the most perplexing enigmas of modern times."

There are some reddish-brown stains found on the cloth correlating, according to proponents, with the wounds in the biblical description of the crucifixion of Jesus. Several years ago, a research team from Texas also did a DNA study of the supposed Shroud bloodstains, but the samples they used were questionable and their results have not been officially recognized. Nevertheless, their findings concluded that the blood on the Shroud is from a male human. Whatever his origin, this male human bears obvious wounds of crucifixion, a practice outlawed in the Roman Empire since the Fourth Century AD. Rivulets of "blood" that encircle the head and the heavy flow on the side recall the biblical crown of thorns and the thrust of the centurion's lance during Christ's Crucifixion. The research team also stated that the blood is so old and degraded that very few DNA segments were found. Since the conclusion of their experiments, other more recent DNA experts with more advanced technology, have argued that so much contamination exists on the Shroud that no DNA test, no matter how carefully done in the future, could ever be considered conclusive or definitive. Today, to avoid further contamination and to protect the Shroud from damage, it is kept inside an airtight box that is 99.5% filled with inert gas argon and .5% oxygen. It is held flat on an aluminum surface. In the past, people were frequently able to view it. Today, however, only on infrequent occasions is it available for viewing, even to those within the hierarchy of the church or the Vatican.

Additionally, modern science has already completed hundreds of thousands of hours of detailed studies and intense research on the Shroud. In 1988, carbon dating appeared to establish that the Shroud was supposedly dated from the Middle Ages, between the years 1260 and 1390. These tests were shown to be suspect for many reasons and may have even been performed on a patch of linen cloth that was sewn onto the Shroud and used to restore it following a fire in a chapel in France where it was kept in the year 1532 AD. The Shroud was subsequently moved from France to the Cathedral in Turin, Italy some 46 years later in the year 1578 AD. For several reasons, the carbon-dating had proven to be both extremely suspect and very inconclusive.

Also, other certain studies declared that the image was "painted on" by a talented medieval artist, or that the type of linen material woven in the cloth did not even exist at the time of Christ's death and resurrection. All these false hypotheses and their resulting "scientific experiments," however, have all since been successfully challenged and subsequently refuted. No pigments, paints, dyes or stains had been found on the linen fibers. Ultra-violet and infrared evaluations had subsequently confirmed the errors present in these studies. What was clear was that there had been a direct contact of the Shroud with an ancient body, which explained certain features such as scourge, thorn, lance, and nail marks, as well as the presence of blood containing hemoglobin. There are blood marks present on the scalp, right chest wall, both wrists and both ankles. However, while this type of contact might explain some of the features of the torso, it is totally incapable of explaining the image of the face with the high resolution that had been amply demonstrated by subsequent photographs. The negative image has a three-dimensional quality and appears to have more likely been produced by something like a burst of intense light or some kind of transient blast of ultra-violet radiation. This left open the possibility of a potential supernatural event being the unknown cause.

All of the arguments which attempt to show that the Shroud of Turin is inauthentic and does not show an image of the dead and subsequently resurrected body of Jesus usually end up by starting with their own preconceived conclusion. They always seem to begin by concluding that there is no way that a person in a dead body can come back to life in a new, glorious, and resurrected body. On the other hand, it cannot be confirmed conclusively that this linen cloth and its image either is or is not, in fact, the actual burial cloth of Jesus. Like the resurrection itself, that remains a complete mystery.

Furthermore, because of the many exhibitions and scientific examinations in the past, any evidence contained on the Shroud may have been contaminated. Through many centuries, the cloth has been handled by countless people, including Church authorities who prepared it for display, the Poor Clare nuns who unstitched portions of it, research teams, scientific experts, visiting dignitaries, and countless others, many of whom have probably left their own DNA on the cloth. Furthermore, the authenticity of the Shroud has historically been a consistent source of debate among scientists, biblical scholars, religious officials, archeologists, historians, and faith-filled believers ever since its discovery. The Shroud has been the property of the Catholic Church since 1980 and has not been on display for several years. Because the overhandling of the Shroud has now become a tremendous cause for concern, this has resulted in church authorities now officially stating that any future research efforts will concentrate exclusively on the preservation and conservation of the Shroud.[2]

Currently the Catholic Church neither formally endorses nor rejects the authenticity of the shroud. Previously, Pope John Paul II had called the Shroud a "distinguished relic" and "a mirror of the Gospel." He has also stated that:

The Shroud is an image of God's love as well as of human sin . . . The imprint left by the tortured body of the Crucified One, which attests to the tremendous human capacity for causing pain and death to one's fellow man, stands as an icon of the suffering of the innocent in every age.[3]

His successor, Pope Benedict XVI, called it an "icon written with the blood of a whipped man, crowned with thorns, crucified, and pierced on his right side." In an inspiring meditation on the Shroud on Holy Saturday in 2010, Pope Benedict had further stated:

> This is the mystery of Holy Saturday! Truly from there, from the darkness of the death of the Son of God, the light of a new hope gleamed: the light of the Resurrection. And it seems to me that, looking at this sacred Cloth through the eyes of faith, one may perceive something of this light. Effectively, the Shroud was immersed in that profound darkness that was at the same time luminous; and I think that if thousands and thousands of people come to venerate it without counting those who contemplate it through images it is because they see in it not only darkness but also the light; not so much the defeat of life and of love, but rather victory, the victory of life over death, of love over hatred. They indeed see the death of Jesus, but they also see his Resurrection.

And further:

> How does the Shroud speak? It speaks with blood, and blood is life! The Shroud is an Icon written in blood; the blood of a man who was scourged, crowned with thorns, crucified and whose right side was pierced. The image impressed upon the Shroud is that of a dead man, but the blood speaks of his life. Every trace of blood speaks of love and of life. Especially that huge stain near his rib, made by the blood and water that flowed copiously from a great wound inflicted by the tip of a Roman spear. That blood and that water speak of life. It is like a spring that murmurs in the silence, and we can hear it, we can listen to it in the silence of Holy Saturday.[4]

In more recent times, Pope Francis has since referred to the Shroud as an "icon of a man scourged and crucified" and his holiness did go on a pilgrimage to Turin in June 2015, to pray before and venerate the Holy Shroud. During the visit to the Cathedral in Turin to pray and reflect before the Shroud, Pope Francis had the following words for those gathered there with him:

> Our thoughts go to the Virgin Mary, a loving, caring mother towards all her children, whom Jesus entrusted to her as He offered Himself on the Cross in the greatest act of love. An icon of this love is the Shroud, which has again drawn so many people to Turin. The Shroud attracts people to the face and tortured body of Jesus and, at the same time, urges us on toward every person who is suffering and unjustly persecuted. It urges us on in the same direction as Jesus' gift of love. The love of Christ urges us on.[5]

Like his predecessors, Pope Francis has certainly neither endorsed nor denied the Shroud's authenticity. However, he has issued carefully worded statements urging the faithful to contemplate the Shroud with deep reverence and awe. Among believers, the mystery of the Shroud inevitably leads one to reflect on the mystery of the resurrection. In no way can it provide anyone with concrete proof of the resurrection. That remains as a matter of faith. On the other hand, the very existence of the Shroud of Turin as a Christian icon has intensified both fervent belief in the resurrection among the Christian faithful as well as having created outright scorn and increased skepticism among the many unbelievers and detractors who doubt the Shroud's authenticity.[6] My own conclusions are that in the end, it should not matter to a Christian believer whether the Shroud is authentic or not. It cannot provide us with any proof of the Resurrection. It is only the Holy Spirit in us, the Spirit of Truth, who can confirm for us that Jesus, our light, is risen. He is made really present to us in the body of Christ through his Living Word, in the Scriptures, and in the Eucharist. Therefore, His promise of our own future bodily resurrection is what we need to firmly believe is truly "authentic" and not necessarily the Shroud.

NOTES

1. "Shroud of Turin, History, Description, & Authenticity, *Encyclopedia Britannica*, https://www.britanica.com/topic/Shroud-of-Turin, also Ibid. Ch. 1 f. 3, see also https://shroudencounter.com/wp-content/uploads/2019/01/WebFact-Sheet-Revised-2014.pdf.
2. Shroud of Turin Education and Research Association, Inc. (STERA, Inc., Florissant, Co.), https://www.shroud.com/; see also National Geographic article 1980 Shroud of Turin http://home.kpn.nl/britso531/Nat.Geographic.June1980.pdf.
3. Pastoral Visit of His Holiness John Paul II to Vercelli and Turin, Italy, 23–24 May 1998. Holy See. 24 May 1998. Pope John Paul II (24 May 1998). Address in Turin Cathedral (Speech). Turin, Italy. Archived from the original on 11 May 2000.
4. Veneration of the Holy Shroud, Meditation of his Holiness, Benedict XVI, Fifth Sunday of Easter, 2 May 2010, https://www.shroud.com/pdfs/Benedict%2002May2010.pdf.
5. Pastoral Visit of His Holiness Pope Francis to Turin, ANGELUS, Piazza Vittorio Sunday, 21 June 2015; https://www.vatican.va/content/francesco/en/angelus/2015/documents/papa-francesco_angelus-torino_20150621.html; see also https://www.theguardian.com/world/2015/jun/21/pope-francis-turin-shroud-icon-of-love.
6. Pope Francis and the Shroud of Turin." *National Catholic Reporter.* 1 April 2013. Retrieved 16 September 2020. "Pope Francis to pray before the Holy Shroud in Turin." Romereports.com. Retrieved 6 June 2016. Pope Francis to Venerate Famed Shroud of Turin in 2015." 6 November 2014. Retrieved 6 June 2016. Pope will visit Shroud of Turin, commemorate birth of St. John Bosco." Ncronlone.org—*National*

Catholic Reporter. 5 November 2014. Retrieved 6 June 2016.). https://www
.ncregister.com/interview/holy-shroud-of-turin-s-authenticity-can-no-longer-be
-disputed-expert-asserts.

Chapter 15

The Catholic Catechism
Dying and Rising

WHAT IS A CATECHISM?

"Catechism" is the name given to a written work that contains a summary of all the beliefs of the faith that is used as a teaching tool. Until the second half of the twentieth century, for millions of Catholics in the United States, the word catechism meant the Baltimore Catechism, which originated in 1884 when the bishops of the United States decided to publish a national catechism. The Baltimore Catechism gave unity to the teaching and understanding of the faith for millions of American Catholics. Its impact was felt right up to the dawn of the Second Vatican Council in 1962. At that time, the Fathers of the Second Vatican Council were charged with guarding and presenting more effectively the deposit of Christian doctrine in order to make it more accessible to the Christian faithful and all people of goodwill in the contemporary world. In 1985, a synod of bishops in Rome convened to celebrate the twentieth anniversary of the conclusion of the Second Vatican Council's proposal to develop a universal catechism. The fruit was the Catechism of the Catholic Church, first published in 1992. The content of the Catechism is faithful to Apostolic Tradition, Scripture, and the Magisterium.[1]

THE CATHOLIC CATECHISM ON RESURRECTION

He Descended into Hell and Rose Again on the Third Day

CC#631 Jesus "descended into the lower parts of the earth. He who descended is he who also ascended far above all the heavens." In the same article, The Apostles' Creed confesses Christ's descent into hell and his Resurrection from the dead on the third day because in his Passover it was precisely out of the depths of death that he made life spring forth:

"Christ, that Morning Star, who came back from the dead, and shed his peaceful light on all mankind, your Son who lives and reigns for ever and ever. Amen."

On the Third Day He Rose from the Dead

CC#638 "We bring you the good news that what God promised to the fathers, this day he has fulfilled to us their children by raising Jesus." The Resurrection of Jesus is the crowning truth of our faith in Christ, a faith believed and lived as the central truth by the first Christian community; handed on as fundamental by Tradition; established by the documents of the New Testament; and preached as an essential part of the Paschal mystery along with the cross:

Christ is risen from the dead! Dying, he conquered death. To the dead, he has given life.

The Historical and Transcendent Event

CC#639 The mystery of Christ's resurrection is a real event, with manifestations that were historically verified, as the New Testament bears witness. In about A.D. 56 St. Paul could already write to the Corinthians: "I delivered to you as of first importance what I also received, that Christ died for our sins in accordance with the scriptures, and that he was buried, that he was raised on the third day in accordance with the scriptures, and that he appeared to Cephas, then to the Twelve . . . " The Apostle speaks here of the living tradition of the Resurrection which he had learned after his conversion at the gates of Damascus.

The Empty Tomb

CC#640 "Why do you seek the living among the dead? He is not here but has risen." The first element we encounter in the framework of the Easter events is the empty tomb. In itself, it is not a direct proof of Resurrection; the absence of Christ's body from the tomb could be explained otherwise. Nonetheless, the empty tomb was still an essential sign for all. Its discovery by the disciples was the first step toward recognizing the very fact of the Resurrection. This was the case, first with the holy women, and then with Peter. The disciple "whom Jesus loved" affirmed that when he entered the empty tomb and discovered "the linen cloths lying there." "he saw and believed." This suggests that he realized from the empty tomb's condition that the absence of Jesus' body could not have been of human doing and that Jesus had not simply returned to earthly life as had been the case with Lazarus.

The Appearance of the Risen One

CC#641 Mary Magdalene and the holy women who came to finish anointing the body of Jesus, which had been buried in haste because the Sabbath began on the evening of Good Friday, were the first to encounter the Risen One. Thus, the women were the first messengers of Christ's Resurrection for the apostles themselves. They were the next to whom Jesus appears: first Peter, then the Twelve. Peter had been called to strengthen the faith of his brothers, and so sees the Risen One before them; it is on the basis of his testimony that the community exclaims: "The Lord has risen indeed and has appeared to Simon!"

CC#642 Everything that happened during those Paschal days involves each of the apostles—and Peter in particular—in the building of the new era begun on Easter morning. As witnesses of the Risen One, they remain the foundation stones of his Church. The faith of the first community of believers is based on the witness of concrete men known to the Christians and for the most part still living among them. Peter and the Twelve are the primary "witnesses to his Resurrection," but they are not the only ones—Paul speaks clearly of more than five hundred persons to whom Jesus appeared on a single occasion and also of James and of all the apostles.

CC#643 Given all these testimonies, Christ's Resurrection cannot be interpreted as something outside the physical order, and it is impossible not to acknowledge it as an historical fact. It is clear from the facts that the disciples' faith was drastically put to the test by their master's Passion and death on the cross, which he had foretold. The shock provoked by the Passion was so great that at least some of the disciples did not at once believe in the news of the Resurrection. Far from showing us a community seized by a mystical exaltation, the Gospels present us with disciples demoralized ("looking sad") and frightened. For they had not believed the holy women returning from the tomb and had regarded their words as an "idle tale." When Jesus reveals himself to the Eleven on Easter evening, "he upbraided them for their unbelief and hardness of heart, because they had not believed those who saw him after he had risen."

CC# 644 Even when faced with the reality of the risen Jesus the disciples are still doubtful, so impossible did the thing seem: they thought they were seeing a ghost. "In their joy they were still disbelieving and still wondering." Thomas will also experience the test of doubt and St. Matthew relates that during the risen Lord's last appearance in Galilee "some doubted." Therefore, the hypothesis that the Resurrection was produced by the apostles' faith (or credulity) will not hold up. On the contrary their faith in the Resurrection was born, under the action of divine grace, from their direct experience of the reality of the risen Jesus.

The Condition of Christ's Risen Humanity

CC#645 By means of touch and the sharing of a meal, the risen Jesus establishes direct contact with his disciples. He invites them in this way to recognize that he is not a ghost and above all to verify that the risen body in which he appears to them is the same body that had been tortured and crucified, for it still bears the traces of his Passion. Yet at the same time this authentic, real body possesses the new properties of a glorious body: not limited by space and time but able to be present how and when he wills; for Christ's humanity can no longer be confined to earth, and belongs henceforth only to the Father's divine realm. For this reason, too, the risen Jesus enjoys the sovereign freedom of appearing as he wishes: in the guise of a gardener or in other forms familiar to his disciples, precisely to awaken their faith.

CC#646 Christ's Resurrection was not a return to earthly life, as was the case with the raisings from the dead that he had performed before Easter: Jairus' daughter, the young man of Naim, and Lazarus. These actions were miraculous events, but the persons miraculously raised returned by Jesus' power to ordinary earthly life. At some particular moment they would die again. Christ's Resurrection is essentially different. In his risen body he passes from the state of death to another life beyond time and space. At Jesus' Resurrection his body is filled with the power of the Holy Spirit: he shares the divine life in his glorious state, so that St. Paul can say that Christ is "the man of heaven."

The Resurrection as a Transcendent Event

CC#647 O truly blessed Night sings the Exultet of the Easter Vigil, which alone deserved to know the time and the hour when Christ rose from the realm of the dead! But no one was an eyewitness to Christ's Resurrection and no evangelist describes it. No one can say how it came about physically. Still less was its innermost essence, his passing over to another life, perceptible to the senses. Although the Resurrection was an historical event that could be verified by the sign of the empty tomb and by the reality of the apostles' encounters with the risen Christ, still it remains at the very heart of the mystery of faith as something that transcends and surpasses history. This is why the risen Christ does not reveal himself to the world, but to his disciples, "to those who came up with him from Galilee to Jerusalem, who are now his witnesses to the people."

The Resurrection—A Work of the Holy Trinity

CC#648 Christ's Resurrection is an object of faith in that it is a transcendent intervention of God himself in creation and history. In it the three divine persons act together as one and manifest their own proper characteristics. The Father's power "raised up" Christ his Son and by doing so perfectly introduced his Son's humanity, including his body, into the Trinity. Jesus is conclusively revealed as "Son of God in power according to the Spirit of holiness by his Resurrection from the dead." St. Paul insists on the manifestation of God's power through the working of the Spirit who gave life to Jesus' dead humanity and called it to the glorious state of Lordship.

CC#649 As for the Son, he effects his own Resurrection by virtue of his divine power. Jesus announces that the Son of man will have to suffer much, die, and then rise. Elsewhere he affirms explicitly: "I lay down my life, that I may take it again . . . I have power to lay it down, and I have power to take it again." "We believe that Jesus died and rose again."

CC#650 The Fathers contemplate the Resurrection from the perspective of the divine person of Christ who remained united to his soul and body, even when these were separated from each other by death: "By the unity of the divine nature, which remains present in each of the two components of man, these are reunited. For as death is produced by the separation of the human components, so Resurrection is achieved by the union of the two."

THE MEANING AND SAVING SIGNIFICANCE OF THE RESURRECTION

CC#651 "If Christ has not been raised, then our preaching is in vain and your faith is in vain." The Resurrection above all constitutes the confirmation of all Christ's works and teachings. All truths, even those most inaccessible to human reason, find their justification if Christ by his Resurrection has given the definitive proof of his divine authority, which he had promised.

CC#652 Christ's Resurrection is the fulfilment of the promises both of the Old Testament and of Jesus himself during his earthly life. The phrase "in accordance with the Scriptures" indicates that Christ's Resurrection fulfilled these predictions.

CC#653 The truth of Jesus' divinity is confirmed by his Resurrection. He had said: "When you have lifted up the Son of man, then you will know that I am he." The Resurrection of the crucified one shows that he was truly

"I AM," the Son of God and God himself. So, St. Paul could declare to the Jews: "What God promised to the fathers, this he has fulfilled to us their children by raising Jesus; as also it is written in the second psalm, 'You are my Son, today I have begotten you.'" Christ's Resurrection is closely linked to the Incarnation of God's Son and is its fulfilment in accordance with God's eternal plan.

CC#654 The Paschal mystery has two aspects: by his death, Christ liberates us from sin; by his Resurrection, he opens for us the way to a new life. This new life is above all justification that reinstates us in God's grace, "so that as Christ was raised from the dead by the glory of the Father, we too might walk in newness of life." Justification consists in both victory over the death caused by sin and a new participation in grace. It brings about filial adoption so that men become Christ's brethren, as Jesus himself called his disciples after his Resurrection: "Go and tell my brethren." We are brethren not by nature, but by the gift of grace, because that adoptive filiation gains us a real share in the life of the only Son, which was fully revealed in his Resurrection.

CC#655 Finally, Christ's Resurrection—and the risen Christ himself is the principle and source of our future resurrection: "Christ has been raised from the dead, the first fruits of those who have fallen asleep . . . For as in Adam all die, so also in Christ shall all be made alive." The risen Christ lives in the hearts of his faithful while they await that fulfilment. In Christ, Christians "have tasted . . . the powers of the age to come" and their lives are swept up by Christ into the heart of divine life, so that they may "live no longer for themselves but for him who for their sake died and was raised."

CATHOLIC CATECHISM ON THE RESURRECTION OF THE BODY

CC#988 The Christian Creed—the profession of our faith in God, the Father, the Son, and the Holy Spirit, and in God's creative, saving, and sanctifying action— culminates in the proclamation of the resurrection of the dead on the last day and in life everlasting.

CC#989 We firmly believe, and hence we hope that, just as Christ is truly risen from the dead and lives forever, so after death the righteous will live forever with the risen Christ, and he will raise them up on the last day. Our resurrection, like his own, will be the work of the Most Holy Trinity:

> If the Spirit of him who raised Jesus from the dead dwells in you, he who raised Christ Jesus from the dead will give life to your mortal bodies also through his Spirit who dwells in you.

CC#990 The term "flesh" refers to man in his state of weakness and mortality. The "resurrection of the flesh" (the literal formulation of the Apostles' Creed) means not only that the immortal soul will live on after death, but that even our "mortal body" will come to life again.

CC#991 Belief in the resurrection of the dead has been an essential element of the Christian faith from its beginnings. "The confidence of Christians is the resurrection of the dead; believing this we live." How can some of you say that there is no resurrection of the dead? But if there is no resurrection of the dead, then Christ has not been raised; if Christ has not been raised, then our preaching is in vain and your faith is in vain. . . . But in fact, Christ has been raised from the dead, the first fruits of those who have fallen asleep.

CHRIST'S RESURRECTION AND OURS

CC#992 God revealed the resurrection of the dead to his people progressively. Hope in the bodily resurrection of the dead established itself as a consequence intrinsic to faith in God as creator of the whole man, soul and body. The creator of heaven and earth is also the one who faithfully maintains his covenant with Abraham and his posterity. It was in this double perspective that faith in the resurrection came to be expressed. In their trials, the Maccabean martyrs confessed:

> The King of the universe will raise us up to an everlasting renewal of life, because we have died for his laws. One cannot but choose to die at the hands of men and to cherish the hope that God gives of being raised again by him.

CC#993 The Pharisees and many of the Lord's contemporaries hoped for the resurrection. Jesus teaches it firmly. To the Sadducees who deny it he answers, "Is not this why you are wrong, that you know neither the scriptures nor the power of God?" Faith in the resurrection rests on faith in God who "is not God of the dead, but of the living."

CC#994 But there is more. Jesus links faith in the resurrection to his own person: "I am the Resurrection and the life." It is Jesus himself who on the last day will raise up those who have believed in him, who have eaten his body and drunk his blood. Already now in this present life he gives a sign and pledge of this by restoring some of the dead to life, announcing thereby his own Resurrection, though it was to be of another order. He speaks of this unique event as the "sign of Jonah," The sign of the temple: he announces that he will be put to death but rise thereafter on the third day.

CC#995 To be a witness to Christ is to be a "witness to his Resurrection," to "[have eaten and drunk] with him after he rose from the dead." Encounters with the risen Christ characterize the Christian hope of resurrection. We shall rise like Christ, with him, and through him.

CC#996 From the beginning, Christian faith in the resurrection has met with incomprehension and opposition. "On no point does the Christian faith encounter more opposition than on the resurrection of the body." It is very commonly accepted that the life of the human person continues in a spiritual fashion after death, but how can we believe that this body, so clearly mortal, could rise to everlasting life?

HOW DO THE DEAD RISE?

CC#997 What is "rising?" In death, the separation of the soul from the body, the human body decays and the soul goes to meet God, while awaiting its reunion with its glorified body. God, in his almighty power, will definitively grant incorruptible life to our bodies by reuniting them with our souls, through the power of Jesus' Resurrection.

CC#998 Who will rise? All the dead will rise, "those who have done good, to the resurrection of life, and those who have done evil, to the resurrection of judgment."

CC#999 How? Christ is raised with his own body: "See my hands and my feet, that it is I myself"; but he did not return to an earthly life. So, in him, "all of them will rise again with their own bodies which they now bear," but Christ "will change our lowly body to be like his glorious body" into a "spiritual body":

> But someone will ask, "How are the dead raised? With what kind of body do they come?" You foolish man! What you sow does not come to life unless it dies. and what you sow is not the body which is to be, but a bare kernel . . . What is sown is perishable, what is raised is imperishable. . . . the dead will be raised imperishable. . . . For this perishable nature must put on the imperishable, and this mortal nature must put on immortality.

CC#1000 This "how" exceeds our imagination and understanding; it is accessible only to faith. Yet our participation in the Eucharist already gives us a foretaste of Christ's transfiguration of our bodies: Just as bread that comes from the earth, after God's blessing has been invoked upon it, is no longer ordinary bread, but Eucharist, formed of two things, the one earthly and the other heavenly—so too our bodies, which partake of the Eucharist are no longer corruptible, but possess the hope of resurrection.

CC#1001 When? Definitively "at the last day," "at the end of the world." Indeed, the resurrection of the dead is closely associated with Christ's Parousia:

> "For the Lord himself will descend from heaven, with a cry of command, with the archangel's call, and with the sound of the trumpet of God. and the dead in Christ will rise first."

RISEN WITH CHRIST

CC#1002 Christ will raise us up "on the last day"; but it is also true that, in a certain way, we have already risen with Christ. For, by virtue of the Holy Spirit, Christian life is already now on earth a participation in the death and Resurrection of Christ:

> And you were buried with him in Baptism, in which you were also raised with him through faith in the working of God, who raised him from the dead . . . If then you have been raised with Christ, seek the things that are above, where Christ is, seated at the right hand of God.

CC#1003 United with Christ by Baptism, believers already truly participate in the heavenly life of the risen Christ, but this life remains "hidden with Christ in God." The Father has already "raised us up with him and made us sit with him in the heavenly places in Christ Jesus." Nourished with his body in the Eucharist, we already belong to the Body of Christ. When we rise on the last day, we "also will appear with him in glory."

CC#1004 In expectation of that day, the believer's body and soul already participate in the dignity of belonging to Christ. This dignity entails the demand that he should treat with respect his own body, but also the body of every other person, especially the suffering:

> The body [is meant] for the Lord, and the Lord for the body. and God raised the Lord and will also raise us up by his power. Do you not know that your bodies are members of Christ?. . . . You are not your own;. . . . So, glorify God in your body.

THE MEMORIAL OF JESUS'S PASSION, DEATH, AND RESURRECTION

The Living Word of God and The Sacrament of the Eucharist

CC#108 The Christian faith is not a "religion of the book." Christianity is the religion of the "Word" of God," a word which is "not a written and mute word, but the Word which is incarnate and living." If the Scriptures are not to remain a dead letter, Christ, the eternal Word of the living God, must, through the Holy Spirit, "open [our] minds to understand the Scriptures."

CC#1322 The holy Eucharist completes Christian initiation. Those who have been raised to the dignity of the royal priesthood by Baptism and configured more deeply to Christ by Confirmation participate with the whole community in the Lord's own sacrifice by means of the Eucharist.

CC#1323 "At the Last Supper, on the night he was betrayed, our Savior instituted the Eucharistic sacrifice of his Body and Blood. This he did in order to perpetuate the sacrifice of the cross throughout the ages until he should come again, and so to entrust to his beloved Spouse, the Church, a memorial of his death and resurrection: a sacrament of love, a sign of unity, a bond of charity, a Paschal banquet 'in which Christ is consumed, the mind is filled with grace, and a pledge of future glory is given to us.'"[2]

NOTES

1. https://www.usccb.org/committees/catechism#:~:text=The%20content%20of %20the%20Catechism,contemporary%20situations%2C%20problems%20and %20questions.

2. https://www.vatican.va/archive/compendium_ccc/documents/archive_2005 _compendium-ccc_en.html#I%20Believe%20in%20the%20Holy%20Spirit; see also https://www.vatican.va/archive/ENG0015/_INDEX.HTM; see also https://www .usccb.org/sites/default/files/flipbooks/catechism/.

Chapter 16

Selected Papal Encyclicals, Letters, and Apostolic Exhortations

Dying and Rising

SELECTED ENCYCLICALS, LETTERS, AND EXHORTATIONS OF POPE JOHN PAUL II ON RESURRECTION

CATECHESI TRADENDAE, On Catechesis in Our Time, Section #9, 1979, John Paul II

In doing so, I am not forgetful that the majesty of Christ the Teacher and the unique consistency and persuasiveness of His teaching can only be explained by the fact that His words, His parables and His arguments are never separable from His life and His very being. Accordingly, the whole of Christ's life was a continual teaching: His silences, His miracles, His gestures, His prayer, His love for people, His special affection for the little and the poor, His acceptance of the total sacrifice on the cross for the redemption of the world, and His resurrection are the actualization of His word and the fulfillment of revelation. Hence for Christians the crucifix is one of the most sublime and popular images of Christ the Teacher.

FAMILIARIS CONSORTIO, Friendly Fellowship, EXHORTATION, #15, 1981, John Paul II

Christian marriage and the Christian family build up the Church: for in the family the human person is not only brought into being and progressively introduced by means of education into the human community, but by means of the rebirth of baptism and education in the faith the child is also introduced into God's family, which is the Church. The human family, disunited by sin, is reconstituted in its unity by the redemptive power of the death and Resurrection of Christ.

FAMILIARIS CONSORTIO, Friendly Fellowship, EXHORTATION, #22, 1981, John Paul II

The sensitive respect of Jesus towards the women that He called to His follow-ing and His friendship, His appearing on Easter morning to a woman before the other disciples, the mission entrusted to women to carry the good news of the Resurrection to the apostles-these are all signs that confirm the special esteem of the Lord Jesus for women.

FAMILIARIS CONSORTIO, Friendly Fellowship, EXHORTATION, #34, 1981, John Paul II

As the Synod noted, this pedagogy embraces the whole of married life. Accordingly, the function of transmitting life must be integrated into the overall mission of Christian life as a whole, which without the Cross cannot reach the Resurrection.

FAMILIARIS CONSORTIO, Friendly Fellowship, EXHORTATION, #39, 1981, John Paul II

By virtue of their ministry of educating, parents are, through the witness of their lives, the first heralds of the Gospel for their children. Furthermore, by praying with their children, by reading the word of God with them and by introduc-ing them deeply through Christian initiation into the Body of Christ-both the Eucharistic and the ecclesial Body-they become fully parents, in that they are begetters not only of bodily life but also of the life that through the Spirit's renewal flows from the Cross and Resurrection of Christ.

FAMILIARIS CONSORTIO, Friendly Fellowship, EXHORTATION, #56, 1981, John Paul II

The sacrament of marriage is the specific source and original means of sancti-fication for Christian married couples and families. It takes up again and makes specific the sanctifying grace of Baptism. By virtue of the mystery of the death and Resurrection of Christ, of which the spouses are made part in a new way by marriage.

FAMILIARIS CONSORTIO, Friendly Fellowship, EXHORTATION, #77, 1981, John Paul II

Similarly, the Church cannot ignore the time of old age, with all its positive and negative aspects. In old age married love, which has been increasingly puri-fied and ennobled by long and unbroken fidelity, can be deepened. There is the opportunity of offering to others, in a new form, the kindness and the wisdom gathered over the years, and what energies remain. But there is also the burden of loneliness, more often psychological and emotional rather than physical, which results from abandonment or neglect on the part of children and relations. There is also suffering caused by ill-health, by the gradual loss of strength, by the humiliation of having to depend on others, by the sorrow of feeling that one is perhaps a burden to one's loved ones, and by the approach of the end of life. These are the circumstances in which, as the Synod Fathers suggested, it is easier to help people understand and live the lofty aspects of the spirituality of marriage and the family, aspects which take their inspiration from the value of Christ's Cross and Resurrection.

RECONCILIATION AND PENANCE, #7, 1984, JOHN PAUL II

Beginning with these and other significant passages in the New Testament, we can therefore legitimately relate all our reflections on the whole mission of Christ to his mission as the one who reconciles. Thus, there must be proclaimed once more the church's belief in Christ's redeeming act, in the paschal mystery of his death and resurrection, as the cause of man's reconciliation in its two-fold aspect of liberation from sin and communion of grace with God.

RECONCILIATION AND PENANCE, #27, 1984, JOHN PAUL II

Baptism is of course a salvific washing which, as St Peter says, is effective "not as a removal of dirt from the body but as an appeal to God for a clear conscience." It is death, burial and resurrection with the dead, buried and risen Christ. It is a gift of the Holy Spirit through Christ.

REDEMPTIONIS DONUM, Redemption Gift, 1984, #12, JOHN PAUL II

This giving is accomplished in the context of the mystery of Christ, who "has made us rich by his poverty." We see how this process of enrichment unfolds in the pages of the Gospel, finding its culmination in the paschal event; Christ, the poorest in His death on the cross, is also the One who enriches us infinitely with the fullness of new life, through the resurrection.

CHRISTIFIDELES LAICI, Mission of the Lay Faithful, Section # 12, 1988, John Paul II

Baptism symbolizes and brings about a mystical but real incorporation into the crucified and glorious body of Christ. Through the sacrament Jesus unites the baptized to his death so as to unite the recipient to his resurrection (cf. Rom 6:3–5).

CHRISTIFIDELES LAICI, Mission of the Lay Faithful, Section # 49, 1988, John Paul II

Though not called to the apostolate of the Twelve, and thereby, to the ministerial priesthood, many women, nevertheless, accompanied Jesus in his ministry and assisted the group of Apostles (cf. Lk 8:2–3), were present at the foot of the Cross (cf. Lk 23:49), assisted at the burial of Christ (cf. Lk 23:55) received and transmitted the message of resurrection on Easter morn (cf. Lk 24:1–10) and prayed with the apostles in the Cenacle awaiting Pentecost (cf. Acts 1:14).

CHRISTIFIDELES LAICI, Mission of the Lay Faithful, Section # 53, 1988, John Paul II

People are called to joy. Nevertheless, each day they experience many forms of suffering and pain. The Synod Fathers in addressing men and women affected by these various forms of suffering and pain used the following words in their final Message: "You who are the abandoned and pushed to the edges of our consumer society; you who are sick, people with disabilities, the poor and hungry, migrants and prisoners, refugees, unemployed, abandoned children and old people who feel alone; you who are victims of war and all kinds of violence: the Church reminds you that she shares your suffering. She takes it to the Lord, who in turn associates you with his redeeming Passion. You are brought to life in the light of his resurrection. We need you to teach the whole world what love is. We will do everything we can so that you may find your rightful place in the Church and in society."

CHRISTIFIDELES LAICI, Mission of the Lay Faithful, Section # 54, 1988, John Paul II

From this perspective the Church has to let the good news resound within a society and culture, which, having lost the sense of human suffering, "censors" all talk on such a hard reality of life. The good news is the proclamation that suffering can even have a positive meaning for the individual and for society itself, since each person is called to a form of participation in the salvific suffering of Christ and in the joy of resurrection, as well as, thereby, to become a force for the sanctification and building up of the Church.

PASTORES DABO VOBIS, I Will Give You Shepherds, EXHORTATION, #13, 1992, John Paul II

Jesus Christ has revealed in himself the perfect and definitive features of the priesthood of the new Covenant. He did this throughout his earthly life, but especially in the central event of his passion, death, and resurrection.

PASTORES DABO VOBIS, I Will Give You Shepherds, EXHORTATION, #25, 1992, John Paul II

After his resurrection, Jesus asked Peter the basic question about love: "Simon, son of John, do you love me more than these?" And following his response Jesus entrusts Peter with the mission: "Feed my lambs" (Jn. 21:15).

APOSTOLIC EXHORTATION, ECCLESIA, The Church IN AFRICA, #32, 1995, John Paul II

Five hundred years ago the people of Angola were added to this chorus of languages. In that moment, in your African homeland the Pentecost of Jerusalem was renewed. Your ancestors heard the message of the Good News which is the language of the Spirit. Their hearts accepted this message for the first time, and they bowed their heads to the waters of the baptismal font in which, by the power of the Holy Spirit, a person dies with Christ and is born again to new life in his Resurrection.

APOSTOLIC EXHORTATION, ECCLESIA, The Church IN AFRICA, #53, 1995, John Paul II

It was precisely when, humanly speaking, Jesus' life seemed doomed to failure that he instituted the Eucharist, "the pledge of eternal glory," in order to perpetuate in time and space his victory over death. That is why at a time when the African Continent is in some ways in a critical situation the Special Assembly for Africa wished to be "the Synod of Resurrection, the Synod of Hope . . . Christ our Hope is alive; we shall live!" Africa is not destined for death, but for life!

APOSTOLIC EXHORTATION, ECCLESIA, The Church IN AFRICA, #83, 1995, John Paul II

Marriage is therefore a state of life, a way of Christian holiness, a vocation which is meant to lead to the glorious resurrection and to the Kingdom, where "they neither marry nor are given in marriage" (Mt 22:30). Marriage thus demands an indissoluble love; thanks to this stability it can contribute effectively to the complete fulfilment of the spouses' baptismal vocation.

EVANGELIUM VITAE, Gospel Life, #29, 1995, John Paul II

As the Second Vatican Council teaches, Christ "perfected revelation by fulfilling it through his whole work of making himself present and manifesting himself; through his words and deeds, his signs and wonders, but especially

through his death and glorious Resurrection from the dead and final sending of
the Spirit of truth.

EVANGELIUM VITAE, Gospel Life, #38, 1995, John Paul II

The life which Jesus gives in no way lessens the value of our existence in time;
it takes it and directs it to its final destiny: "I am the resurrection and the life . . .
whoever lives and believes in me shall never die" (Jn 11:25–26).

EVANGELIUM VITAE, Gospel Life, #97, 1995, John Paul II

Death itself is anything but an event without hope. It is the door which opens
wide on eternity and, for those who live in Christ, an experience of participation
in the mystery of his Death and Resurrection.

EVANGELIUM VITAE, Gospel Life, #105, 1995, John Paul II

"Death shall be no more" (Rev 21:4): the splendor of the Resurrection . . .
"Death with life contended: combat strangely ended! Life's own Champion,
slain, yet lives to reign."

APOSTOLIC EXHORTATION, ECCLESIA, The Church, IN AMERICA, #75, 1999, John Paul II

"I am with you always, to the end of the age" (Mt 28:20). Trusting in this promise of the Lord, the pilgrim Church in America prepares enthusiastically to meet
the challenges of today's world and those that will come in the future. In the
Gospel, the Good News of the Resurrection of the Lord is accompanied by the
invitation to fear not (cf. Mt 28:5, 10).

APOSTOLIC EXHORTATION, ECCLESIA, The Church, IN ASIA, #2, 1999, John Paul II

If the Church in Asia is to fulfil its providential destiny, evangelization as the
joyful, patient and progressive preaching of the saving Death and Resurrection
of Jesus Christ must be your absolute priority.

APOSTOLIC EXHORTATION, ECCLESIA, The Church IN ASIA, #11, 1999, John Paul II

Through his words and actions, especially in his suffering, death and resurrection, Jesus fulfilled the will of his Father to reconcile all humanity to himself, after original sin had created a rupture in the relationship between the Creator and his creation. On the Cross, he took upon himself the sins of the world—past, present and future.

APOSTOLIC EXHORTATION, ECCLESIA, The Church IN ASIA, #13, 1999, John Paul II

How does the humanity of Jesus and the ineffable mystery of the Incarnation of the Son of the Father shed light on the human condition? The Incarnate Son of God not only revealed completely the Father and his plan of salvation; he also "fully reveals man to himself." His words and actions, and above all his Death and Resurrection, reveal the depths of what it means to be human.

APOSTOLIC EXHORTATION, ECCLESIA, The Church IN ASIA, #17, 1999, John Paul II

The Holy Spirit preserves unfailingly the bond of communion between Jesus and his Church. . . . Empowered by the Spirit to accomplish Christ's salvation on earth, the Church is the seed of the Kingdom of God and she looks eagerly for its final coming. Her identity and mission are inseparable from the Kingdom of God which Jesus announced and inaugurated in all that he said and did, above all in his death and resurrection.

APOSTOLIC EXHORTATION, ECCLESIA, The Church IN OCEANIA, #5, 2001, John Paul II

When Christ dwelt among us, he proclaimed the Good News that God's Kingdom has come, a Kingdom of peace, justice, and truth. Many people, particularly from among the poor, the needy and the outcast, followed him, but for the most part the powerful of the world turned against him. They condemned him and nailed him to the Cross. This shameful death, accepted by the Father as a sacrifice of love for the world's sake, gave way to a glorious Resurrection by the power of the Father's love.

APOSTOLIC EXHORTATION, ECCLESIA, The Church IN EUROPE, #48 & 49, 2003, John Paul II

If our hope is to be true and unshakable, "an integral, clear and renewed preaching of the Risen Christ, the resurrection and eternal life" must be a priority for pastoral activity in coming years . . . Europe calls out for credible evangelizers, whose lives, in communion with the Cross and Resurrection of Christ, radiate the beauty of the Gospel. Such evangelizers must be properly trained.

PASTORES GREGIS, Shepherds of the Flock, EHORTATION, #27, 2003, JOHN PAUL II

The proclamation of the Lord's death and Resurrection thus includes "the prophetic proclamation of a hereafter, which is man's deepest and definitive calling, in continuity and discontinuity with his present situation: beyond time and history, beyond the reality of this world, which is passing away.'"

SELECTED ENCYCLICALS, LETTERS, AND EXHORTATIONS OF POPE BENEDICT XVI ON RESURRECTION

CARITAS IN VERITATE, Charity in Truth, 2009, #1, Benedict XVI

Charity in truth, to which Jesus Christ bore witness by his earthly life and especially by his death and resurrection, is the principal driving force behind the authentic development of every person and of all humanity. Love—caritas—is an extraordinary force which leads people to opt for courageous and generous engagement in the field of justice and peace. It is a force that has its origin in God, Eternal Love and Absolute Truth.

SPE SALVI, Saved Through Hope, 2007, # 41, Benedict XVI

At the conclusion of the central section of the Church's great Credo—the part that recounts the mystery of Christ, from his eternal birth of the Father and his temporal birth of the Virgin Mary, through his Cross and Resurrection to the second coming—we find the phrase: "he will come again in glory to judge the living and the dead.

SPE SALVI, Saved Through Hope, 2007, #42, Benedict XVI

He also constantly emphasized this "negative" dialectic and asserted that justice—true justice—would require a world "where not only present suffering would be wiped out, but also that which is irrevocably past would be undone" [30]. This, would mean, however—to express it with positive and hence, for him, inadequate symbols—that there can be no justice without a resurrection of the dead. Yet this would have to involve "the resurrection of the flesh, something that is totally foreign to idealism and the realm of Absolute spirit."

SPE SALVI, Saved Through Hope, 2007, #43, Benedict XVI

God now reveals his true face in the figure of the sufferer who shares man's God-forsaken condition by taking it upon himself. This innocent sufferer has attained the certitude of hope: there is a God, and God can create justice in a way that we cannot conceive, yet we can begin to grasp it through faith. Yes, there is a resurrection of the flesh [33]. There is justice [34]. There is an "undoing" of past suffering, a reparation that sets things aright.

SPE SALVI, Saved Through Hope, 2007, #44, Benedict XVI

In the parable of the rich man and Lazarus (cf. Lk 16:19–31), Jesus admonishes us through the image of a soul destroyed by arrogance and opulence, who has created an impassable chasm between himself and the poor man; the chasm of being trapped within material pleasures; the chasm of forgetting the other, of incapacity to love, which then becomes a burning and unquenchable thirst. We must note that in this parable Jesus is not referring to the final destiny after the Last Judgement, but is taking up a notion found, inter alia, in early Judaism, namely that of an intermediate state between death and resurrection, a state in which the final sentence is yet to be pronounced.

SPE SALVI, Saved Through Hope, 2007, #50, Benedict XVI

"Do not be afraid, Mary!" In that hour at Nazareth the angel had also said to you: "Of his kingdom there will be no end" (Lk 1:33). Could it have ended before it began? No, at the foot of the Cross, on the strength of Jesus's own word, you became the mother of believers. In this faith, which even in the darkness of Holy Saturday bore the certitude of hope, you made your way towards Easter morning. The joy of the Resurrection touched your heart and united you in a new way to the disciples, destined to become the family of Jesus through faith.

DEUS CARITAS EST, God is Love, 2005, #6, Benedict XVI

"Whoever seeks to gain his life will lose it, but whoever loses his life will preserve it" (Lk 17:33), as Jesus says throughout the Gospels (cf. Mt 10:39; 16:25; Mk 8:35; Lk 9:24; Jn 12:25). In these words, Jesus portrays his own path, which leads through the Cross to the Resurrection: the path of the grain of wheat that falls to the ground and dies, and in this way bears much fruit.

DEUS CARITAS EST, God is Love, 2005, #13, Benedict XVI

Jesus gave this act of oblation an enduring presence through his institution of the Eucharist at the Last Supper. He anticipated his death and resurrection by giving his disciples, in the bread and wine, his very self, his body and blood as the new manna. (cf. Jn 6:31–33)

DEUS CARITAS EST, God is Love, 2005, #19, Benedict XVI

By dying on the Cross—as Saint John tells us—Jesus "gave up his Spirit" (Jn 19:30), anticipating the gift of the Holy Spirit that he would make after his Resurrection (cf. Jn 20:22). This was to fulfil the promise of "rivers of living water" that would flow out of the hearts of believers, through the outpouring of the Spirit (cf. Jn 7:38–39).

SACRAMENTUM CARITATIS, The Sacrament of Charity, 2007, #10, Benedict XVI

The institution of the Eucharist took place within a ritual meal commemorating the foundational event of Israel, its deliverance from slavery in Egypt. This is the context in which Jesus introduces the newness of his gift. In instituting the Eucharist, Jesus anticipates and makes present the sacrifice of the Cross and the victory of the resurrection, revealing himself as the true sacrificial lamb. Jesus thus shows the salvific meaning of his death and resurrection, a mysterious renewal of history and the whole universe.

SACRAMENTUM CARITATIS, The Sacrament of Charity, 2007, #22, Benedict XVI

The relationship between these two sacraments becomes clear in situations of serious illness: "In addition to the Anointing of the Sick, the Church offers those who are about to leave this life the Eucharist as viaticum." (67) On their journey to the Father, communion in the Body and Blood of Christ appears as the seed of eternal life and the power of resurrection: "Anyone who eats my flesh and drinks my blood has eternal life and I will raise him up on the last day" (Jn 6:54).

SACRAMENTUM CARITATIS, The Sacrament of Charity, 2007, #32, Benedict XVI

The Eucharistic celebration is a pledge of future glory. Celebrating the memorial of our salvation strengthens our hope in the resurrection of the body and of meeting once again, face to face, those who have died, marked with the sign of faith.

SACRAMENTUM CARITATIS, The Sacrament of Charity, 2007, #35, Benedict XVI

In the New Testament this epiphany of beauty reaches absolute fulfillment in God's revelation in Jesus Christ, the full manifestation of the glory of God. Jesus Christ transformed the dark mystery of death into the radiant light of the resurrection.

SACRAMENTUM CARITATIS, The Sacrament of Charity, 2007, #92, Benedict XVI

The relationship between the Eucharist and the universe helps us to see the unity of God's plan, to grasp the profound relationship between creation and the "new creation" inaugurated in the resurrection of Christ.[2]

SELECTED ENCYCLICALS, LETTERS, AND EXHORTATIONS OF POPE FRANCIS ON RESURRECTION

EVANGELII GAUDIUM, The Joy of the Gospel, 2013, #3, Pope Francis

No one can strip us of the dignity bestowed upon us by this boundless and unfailing love. With a tenderness which never disappoints, but is always capable of restoring our joy, he makes it possible for us to lift up our heads and to start anew. Let us not flee from the resurrection of Jesus, let us never give up, come what will. May nothing inspire more than his life, which impels us onwards!

EVANGELII GAUDIUM, The Joy of the Gospel, 2013, #276, Pope Francis

Christ's resurrection is not an event of the past; it contains a vital power which has permeated this world. Where all seems to be dead, signs of the Resurrection suddenly spring up. It is an irresistible force. . . . Each day in our world beauty is born anew, it rises transformed through the storms of history. Values always tend to reappear under new guises, and human beings have arisen time after time from situations that seemed doomed. Such is the power of the resurrection, and all who evangelize are instruments of that power.

EVANGELII GAUDIUM, The Joy of the Gospel, 2013, #277, Pope Francis

It also happens that our hearts can tire of the struggle because in the end we are caught up in ourselves, in a careerism which thirsts for recognition, applause, rewards and status. In this case we do not lower our arms, but we no longer grasp what we seek, the resurrection is not there. In cases like these, the Gospel, the most beautiful message that this world can offer, is buried under a pile of excuses.

EVANGELII GAUDIUM, The Joy of the Gospel, 2013, #278, Pope Francis

The kingdom is here, it returns, it struggles to flourish anew. Christ's resurrection everywhere calls forth seeds of that new world; even if they are cut back, they grow again, for the resurrection is already secretly woven into the fabric of this history, for Jesus did not rise in vain. May we never remain on the sidelines of this march of living hope!

LUMEN FIDEI, The Light of Faith, 2013, #18, Pope Francis

To enable us to know, accept and follow him, the Son of God took on our flesh. Christian faith is faith in the incarnation of the Word and his bodily resurrection. It is faith in a God so close to us that he entered our human history.

LUMEN FIDEI, The Light of Faith, 2013, #20, Pope Francis

Faith's new way of seeing things is centered on Christ. Faith in Christ brings salvation because our lives become radically open to a love that precedes and transforms us from within. Paul interprets the nearness of God's word in terms of Christ's presence in the Christian. Christ came down to earth and rose from the dead. By his Incarnation and resurrection, the son of God embraced the whole of human life and history. He now dwells in our hearts through the Holy Spirit.

LUMEN FIDEI, The Light of Faith, 2013, #54, Pope Francis

At the heart of biblical faith is God's love, his concrete concern for every person and his plan of salvation for all of humanity, culminating in the incarnation, death and resurrection of Jesus Christ.

LAUDATO SI, On the Care of Our Common Home, 2015, #83, Pope Francis

The ultimate destiny of the universe is in the fullness of God, which has already been attained by the risen Christ, the measure of the maturity of all things. Here we can add yet another argument for rejecting every tyrannical and irresponsible domination of human beings over other creatures. The ultimate purpose of other creatures is not to be found in us. Rather, all creatures are moving forward, with us and through us, towards a common point of arrival, which is God, in that transcendent fullness where the risen Christ embraces and illumines all things.

LAUDATO SI, On the Care of Our Common Home, 2015, #100, Pope Francis

The New Testament does not only tell us of the earthly Jesus and his tangible and loving relationship with the world. It also shows him risen and glorious, present throughout creation by his universal Lordship.

LAUDATO SI, On the Care of Our Common Home, 2015, #237, Pope Francis

On Sunday, our participation in the Eucharist has special importance. Sunday, like the Jewish Sabbath, is meant to be a day which heals our relationships, with God, with ourselves, with others and with the world. Sunday is the day of the Resurrection, the "first day" of the new creation, whose first fruits are the Lord's risen humanity, the pledge of the final transfiguration of all created reality.

LAUDATO SI, On the Care of Our Common Home, 2015, #241, Pope Francis

Mary, the Mother who cared for Jesus, now cares with maternal affection and pain for this wounded world. Just as her transfixed heart mourned the death of Jesus, so now she grieves for the sufferings of the crucified poor and for the creatures of this world laid waste by human power. Completely transfigured, she now lives with Jesus, and all creatures sing of her fairness. She is the Woman, "clothed in the sun, with the moon under her feet, and on her head a crown of twelve stars" (Rev 12:1). Carried up into heaven, she is the Mother and Queen of all creation. In her glorified body, together with the Risen Christ, part of creation has reached the fullness of its beauty.

FRATELLI TUTTI, Brothers All, 2020, #278, Pope Francis

For many Christians, this journey of fraternity also has a Mother, whose name is Mary. Having received this universal motherhood at the foot of the cross (cf. Jn 19:26), she cares not only for Jesus but also for "the rest of her children" (cf. Rev 12:17). In the power of the risen Lord, she wants to give birth to a new world, where all of us are brothers and sisters, where there is room for all those whom our societies discard, where justice and peace are resplendent.

FRATELLI TUTTI, Brothers All, 2020, #287, Conclusion, In a Prayer to the Creator, Pope Francis

Grant that we Christians may live the Gospel,
discovering Christ in each human being,
recognizing him crucified
in the sufferings of the abandoned
and forgotten of our world,
and risen in each brother or sister
who makes a new start.[3]

NOTES

1. Encyclicals, Apostolic Exhortations, Letters, Documents, Pope John Paul II, on Resurrection, https://www.vatican.va/offices/papal_docs_list.html.

2. Encyclicals, Apostolic Exhortations, Letters, Documents, Pope Benedict XVI, on Resurrection, https://www.vatican.va/offices/papal_docs_list.html.

3. Encyclicals, Apostolic Exhortations, Letters, Documents, Pope Francis, on Resurrection, https://www.vatican.va/offices/papal_docs_list.html.

Chapter 17

The Risen Christ Is the
Universal Christ

NEW TESTAMENT

The Old Testament of the Bible had established a close bond between Yahweh as God and the universe. Beginning with the creation account in the Book of Genesis, this bond then extends throughout many of the Psalms, Wisdom Books, and the Prophets. We find several references to this, for example, in the Book of the Prophet Jeremiah (Jer. 4:23–36, 5:22–23, 9:9, 10:10, 27:5–6).

In the New Testament, The Universal Christ can best be described as that aspect of the exalted and eternal God in the Risen Christ which fills the entire universe and is limitless to time and space. Because of the trans-historical character of the resurrection of Christ, the Universal Christ would have no bounds or limits in the historical process. On the one hand, the resurrection could be termed "a historical event" because it took place in a precise context at a particular time and place. It was also an event which Christ had foretold. In addition to that, the women who were disciples had found the tomb empty and were told, "He has risen as he said" (Matt. 28:5–6). There were also many post resurrection appearances to many people at certain times and places. For these people the resurrection could only be historical. Furthermore, it is true that Jesus invited the disciples to touch his risen body to confirm his identity. These different factors provide us with some evidential proofs of the historicity of the risen Christ, but, on the other hand, the resurrection overarches all of history as a unique supernatural event. Thus, we are reminded by the words of the late Pope John Paul II who has told us that:

> The resurrection transcends and stands above history . . . No one was an eyewitness to the resurrection . . . No one could say how it had happened in reality . . .

Our senses could never perceive Jesus' passage to another life . . . It is this trans-historical feature of the resurrection that must be especially considered if we are to understand to some extent the mystery of that historical, but also trans-historical event.[1]

The risen Christ as the Universal Christ is perfecting the universe throughout the entire span of history. The intimate link between Christ and the perfection of the historical universe is justified on New Testament grounds by the victory Christ won through his death on the cross and resurrection as all the forces controlling the universe were made subject to him. In his person, all cohesive power in the history of the universe was centered in Christ. Following his resurrection, Jesus Christ received his full role as Lord (Kyrios) of the entire universe.[2]

New Testament references to the resurrected Christ being preeminent and having become The Universal Christ can be found primarily in the Gospel of John as well as in Paul's Letter to the Colossians and his Letter to the Ephesians:

I. The Preeminence of the Risen and Universal Christ

In the beginning was the Word, and the Word was with God, and the Word was God. He was in the beginning with God. All things came to be through him, and without him nothing came to be. What came to be through him was life, and this life was the light of the human race. The light shines in the darkness and the darkness has not overcome it. (Jn. 1:1–5)

II. The Preeminence of the Risen and Universal Christ

He is the image of the invisible God, the firstborn of all creation. For in him were created all things in heaven and on earth, the visible and the invisible, whether thrones or dominions or principalities or powers; all things were created through him and for him. He is before all things, and in him all things hold together. He is the head of the body, the church. He is the beginning, the firstborn from the dead, that in all things he himself might be preeminent. For in him, all the fullness was pleased to dwell, and through him to reconcile all things for him, making peace by the blood of his cross [through him] whether those on earth or those in heaven. (Col. 1:15–20)

III. The Preeminence of the Risen and Universal Christ

He has made known to us the mystery of his will in accord with his favor that he set forth in him as a plan for the fullness of times, to sum up all things in Christ, in heaven and on earth. And what is the surpassing greatness of his power for us who believe, in accord with the exercise of his great might, which he worked in Christ, raising him from the dead and seating him at his right hand in the heavens, far above every principality, authority, power, and dominion, and every name that is named not only in this age but also in the one to come. And he put all things beneath his feet and gave him as head over all things to the church, which is his body, the fullness of the one who fills all things in every way. And to bring to light [for all] what is the plan of the mystery hidden from ages past in God who created all things, so that the manifold wisdom of God might now be made known through the church to the principalities and authorities in the heavens. (Eph. 1:9–10, 19–23; 3:9–10)[3]

The above three New Testament references affirming the Resurrected Christ as the Universal Christ were also reaffirmed in the early Christian church through the writings of the Church Fathers, Ignatius of Antioch, Clement, and Irenaeus. The theology of the Universal Christ can also be found in the Middle-Ages in the writings of Thomas Aquinas and Bonaventure and in our current day in the theologies of Vatican Council II, and more specifically in the theologies of Jesuits, Pierre Teilhard de Chardin and Karl Rahner, as well as the writings of Franciscan priest and author, Fr. Richard Rohr.

THE RESURRECTION OF CHRIST AND THE HISTORY OF THE UNIVERSE

Many Christians believe that with the Incarnation of Jesus Christ, the history of the universe has entered its final phase. Jesus of Nazareth after his crucifixion and resurrection has become The Universal Christ. Therefore, the universe, past, present, and future has been divinized and spiritized. Because it occurred on the other side of death, the resurrection of Christ cannot be viewed as something fully historical in every sense of the word as it is something impacting everyone and everything in the universe throughout all space and time. This could only occur through the grace of God which implies that it can only be perceived as reality grounded in mystery.

Reality is the quality or state of being real, genuine, and authentic. It has a basis in fact and truth. It includes everything that is, no matter whether observable or comprehensible, visible, or invisible. Reality is far more complex than what our immediate sense experience can tell us. The senses of seeing, hearing, tasting, touching, and smelling provide us with our immediate sense experience, but reality and the criteria for what is considered as "real" in the universe is mediated by meaning. Because reality is dynamic and mediated by meaning, what occurs is that reality can constantly change as meaning changes over time. This gives to history not only a past and present, but also a future dimension. Therefore, it is mystery which is the ground of all reality. When we view any event in the historical process, we need to be open to our not grasping either its complete reality or its full meaning. This would include the resurrection of Jesus Christ as well as our own future bodily resurrection.[4]

Jesuit theologians Karl Rahner and Pierre Teilhard de Chardin might describe this as historical consciousness moving from lower to higher, from matter to spirit, and moving from unconsciousness to consciousness to self-consciousness, to Christ-consciousness. Everything in the universe past, present, and future is in a state of becoming. The history of the universe has become inextricably intertwined with the ongoing history of the body of Christ. The crucifixion and death of Christ is certainly an historical event. But all of history has now been, is, or will be unified and threaded with the resurrection event as well. This universal Christ-consciousness is possible only because of the self-communication of God in grace. Through the resurrection, God who is Holy Mystery is present to reality in grace. In the rising of Christ, this grace is not merely communicated by God; it IS God.[5]

THE UNIVERSE AND ALL OF HISTORY
IS CHRISTOCENTRIC

In its most simple definition, "Christocentrism" indicates that the human personhood assumed by The Son of God in the Incarnation is a mystery which will bring about the radical renewal of creation, the salvation of humankind, and the ultimate perfection of the universe through the power of love. Following the death and resurrection of Jesus Christ, history entered its final phase and became Christocentric in that Christ was, is, and will be the beginning, the center, and the end goal of all human existence and of the entire history of the universe. The universe with Christ as its head is the true end and essence of Christianity, in that all things are now permeated with the special presence of God throughout the history of the universe. The Word spoken into the universe is Christ, and our own reality is tied up with the same reality as the universality of Christ in history. In Pierre Teilhard de Chardin's landmark book, The *Phenomenon of Man*, he points out that the universe in terms of the historical process is in dynamic movement to its highest end-point, "The Omega Point," which he equates with the Universal or Cosmic Christ. The Resurrected Christ is the Universal Christ and the Omega Point is the time and place where the cosmos intersects with God in the Universal Christ, making the entire history of the universe Christocentric. At this intersection, Teilhard envisioned an interplay of what he called the two convergences—the cosmic (natural) and the Christic (supernatural).

Furthermore, because of "Christ in us," through and with the dynamism of the Holy Spirit as the power of our self-transcendence (and because the Holy Spirit always points to Christ)—all of our destinies are tied up with the Universal Christ at this meeting point of the universe with Christ. God the Father who created the universe, the crucified and risen Christ, and the Holy Spirit in us is what makes the history of the universe Christocentric. It will bring about ultimate reality and meaning, not only for the whole of the historical universe, but for us personally as well. In the crucified and risen Christ, the universal and the personal are being drawn into oneness.[6]

THE RISEN CHRIST IS THE UNIVERSAL CHRIST

Before time began, while silence encompassed the universe, the Infinite Word was in the bosom of the Eternal Father to be spoken into the universe and become incarnate in the fullness of time. Even after the Word was spoken and made flesh, He would always remain inseparable from the Father and The Holy Spirit. As we continue to discuss The Universal Christ, it should be stated explicitly here that we certainly should not leave behind the Jesus of history in envisioning the Resurrected Christ as the Universal Christ in the historical process. So, I would like to quote the words of that brilliant Jesuit theologian, Pierre Teilhard de Chardin whom we briefly mentioned above:

> The Universal Christ has neither meaning nor value in our eyes except as an expansion of the Christ who was born of Mary and died on the cross.[7]

It is marvelous to consider that The Universal Christ, the Lord of the Cosmos, was once enclosed in the loving womb of his mother and that at one time in history, Jesus's known universe was Mary's womb. The title of "Christ" is not part of Jesus's name. The title confers upon Jesus a universal role that is greater than even Christianity itself as a world religion. Christ is a translation of the Hebrew word *Masiah*—Messiah and was a title which came from the Greek word, *Christos*, which means "Anointed One." Following his crucifixion, death, resurrection, and ascension, (seen as one event), Jesus of Nazareth would then be considered "The Universal Christ." The early Christian community, in believing that Jesus Christ was the Son of God, also conferred upon him the title *Kyrios* which was the Greek translation for "Lord" or "God." This word appears seven hundred times in the New Testament. Also, the word "catholic" simply means "universal," and when used in religious matters, the term is generally capitalized. "Catholic" was first used by the church Father, Ignatius of Antioch, in 110 AD.[8]

The Universal Christ can also be seen as the life and love principle of everything in the universe. Therefore, we should make a conscious choice to see God in everyone, in everything, and everywhere. In being universal, Jesus Christ no longer belongs to any particular age, nation, or religion. As stated earlier, one cannot affirm The Universal Christ without affirming Jesus of Nazareth. To do this would make the risen Christ only a cosmic idea or some mythical icon. That being said, Jesus of Nazareth, in his life and death on the cross, can be called a person of recorded history as we know it. But there were no actual witnesses to the resurrection as it happened. As regards the resurrection itself, recorded history is silent. This leaves a question as to whether Jesus's resurrection, when restricted as it is to empty tomb and appearance stories in the Bible, should be viewed as an historical event at all. However, if one believes that the Resurrection of Jesus of Nazareth is the Christocentric point in which He became the Universal Christ, then it becomes more than simply an event to be viewed through the lens of recorded history as we know it. Rather, it would make this event something "trans-historical," in that the resurrection of Jesus Christ from the dead would then have a dynamic bearing on both our individual lives as well as the past, present, and future of the entire span of the historical universe. Although "History" can often be seen as an umbrella term comprising only the examination, analyzing, and recording of past events, it should also take into account the various collective memories and differing interpretations of these events because oftentimes no one narrative can best explain the significance of any event. This would be the case particularly if the event is seen to have occurred on the other side of death and beyond the confines of time and space.

The New Testament letter to the Hebrews opens with a reflection on the climax of God's revelation to the human race through his Son, Jesus Christ. The divine communication was initiated and maintained during Old Testament times in fragmentary and varied ways through the prophets, including Abraham, Moses, and all persons and prophets through whom God spoke. But now in these last days, the final age, God's revelation of his saving purpose is achieved through one who is God's Son, whose role is redeemer and mediator of all of creation. Jesus Christ has been made heir of all things through his death and resurrection. Yet he existed before he appeared as man, and through him God created the entire universe. The Word became flesh and now Christ is risen. There are no more words and there is only the silence of God which remains for us to hear in prayer. The Letter to the Hebrews opens with these two verses:

In times past, God spoke in partial and various ways to our ancestors through the prophets; in these last days, he spoke to us through a Son, whom he made heir of all things and through whom he created the universe. (Heb. 1:1–2)[9]

Finally, as was stated earlier, what is most personal is most universal, and what is most universal is most personal. Therefore, the universal must be made personal within us. The New Testament tells us that following his crucifixion death, and resurrection, Christ sent the Holy Spirit from the Father. By virtue of our Baptism, the eternal is in us and should point to Christ. Therefore, we have become part of both the Body of Christ and the evolving Christocentric universe. As Christians, our participation in both the Body of Christ and the Christocentric Universe is what should give us our ultimate purpose and meaning in all of reality. However, God is love (1 Jn. 4:8,16); love is expansive and never ends, and reality is dynamic and not static. Therefore, neither we, as loving persons nor the Christocentric universe, are simply static realities of being in the historical process. Both we and the Christocentric universe are always and continually in the process of evolving and dynamically becoming. Christ has risen, is Lord of the universe, and waits for us now at the Omega Point of history. Meanwhile, the historical universe and each one of us who is attempting to follow the rising light of Christ leading the way to our own bodily resurrection on the other side of death, must be abiding, evolving, and becoming somewhere between the "already" and "not yet" of Eternal Life.[10]

NOTES

1. Online https://www.ewtn.com/catholicism/library/resurrection-is-a-historical -event-that-transcends-history-24199.
2. Ibid. Ch. 3 f. 1. (See Jerome Biblical Commentary, Sec. 55:1–9 p. 335). See also Pope John Paul II, General Audience, 3/1/1989, http://www.totus2us.co.uk/ teaching/jpii-catechesis-on-god-the-son-jesus/the-resurrection-is-a-historical-event -that-transcends-history/.
3. Ibid. Ch. 1 f. 3; see also M. Hickey, *Holy Silence* (Lanham, Md., Hamilton Books, 2022, pp. 111–118).
4. Hickey, Michael, *Get Real, Reality and Mystery,* (Lanham, Md., University Press, 2012, pp. 1–30).
5. Ibid Ch. 13 f. 17, see also "Grace," R. McBrien, *Catholicism* (New York, NY, Harper & Co., 1966, pp. 171–188)
6. "The Omega Point," De Chardin, Pierre Teilhard, *Phenomenon of Man,* (New York, NY, Harper & Co., 1965, pp. 257–298).
7. De Chardin, Pierre Teilhard, *Divine Milieu* (New York, NY, Harper Perennial., 1964, p. 117).
8. "Catholic/ Catholic," Ignatius of Antioch, *Letter to the Smyrnaeans*, online https://www.catholic.com/magazine/online-edition/apologetics-with-st-ignatius-of -antioch, see also https://www.newadvent.org/cathen/07644a.htm

9. Ibid. Ch. 1 f. 3.

10. "Omega Point," Ibid. Ch. 17, f. 5, see also "Kingdom of God," R. McBrien, *Catholicism* (New York, NY, Harper & Co., 1966, p. 1243)

Chapter 18

Humor as a Signal of Transcendence and a Sign of Resurrection

HUMOR AS A SIGNAL OF TRANSCENDENCE

As a grad student at Weston/Boston College School of Theology and Ministry, I once had the opportunity to cross register for a course at Boston University through membership in the Boston Theological Institute. I wanted to take a course with Dr. Peter Berger. He was a well-known theologian and sociologist who, in the face of the "God is dead" movement of the 1960s, argued that faith can flourish in modern society if people learn to recognize the transcendent in ordinary experiences. Dr. Berger had written a book I found most interesting and enlightening. The title of the book was *Rumor of Angels*. The subtitle of the book indicated that it was "Modern Society's Rediscovery of the Supernatural." The book and the course involved a study of what Dr. Berger called "Signals of Transcendence," and *Rumor of Angels* was the course-study book used for that course as I pursued my M-Div. degree from Weston/Boston College.[1]

Dr. Berger outlined five signals of transcendence in his book. The last one was the signal of transcendence that I found the most intriguing and that was the "Argument from Humor." In his book, Dr. Berger had written the following:

A situation is invariably comic when it belongs simultaneously to two altogether independent series of events and is capable of being interpreted in two entirely different meanings at the same time.[2]

I should state at this point that I did my final term paper for the course on the subject of humor as a signal of transcendence attempting to expand on Dr. Berger's thoughts on humor. I wanted to show how in addition to humor being a signal of transcendence, it was also in some ways a sign of resurrection. The paper I felt was in depth and insightful, but the one mistake I may have made was paraphrasing the title of my paper around the title of his book *Rumor of Angels,* and titling the term paper, A *Rumor of Humor.* In it, I wanted to show that humor certainly was a signal of transcendence, but also was something that the divine put deep into the very nature of man as grace and was a part of man's very created being. Humor is thoroughly human. One need not look first to the angels to find the hand of God present in humor. For the previous three years, I had been schooled in theology as being a "Transcendental Anthropology." This was the theology of Jesuit Karl Rahner, whom most Catholic scholars and theologians are familiar with (see chapter 11 of this book). Transcendental Anthropology begins with the human person and then attempts to find the presence of the transcendent divine in every created being and all created things.[3] In this method, any theological study of humor would begin with man, the human. In fact, I said I believed that God gave us humor as a way of realizing that God has a sense of humor. If you doubt this at all and want to hear God laugh, just tell him what your plan is for your life. I also wanted to show that in some ways, humor was a sign of resurrection. Even though he gave me a B grade, I think he really did not appreciate the paraphrasing of my title based on his book title and may have even taken it as a personal affront. My sense at the completion of the course was that Dr. Berger (who has since passed) was a very intelligent man and a brilliant Protestant theologian, but even though he had a sense of humor, it probably was not his greatest asset. Furthermore, Dr. Berger didn't show much appreciation for the theology of Jesuit Karl Rahner and his Transcendental Anthropology which I considered simply profound and became the basis for much of my own evolving theological thought processes. A few years later, I wrote a book on virtues in 2011 titled, *Get Goodness*, where I discussed some 50 virtues, one of which was the virtue of "Humor."[4] This furthered my initial interest in wanting to explore and write about humor as a signal of transcendence beginning with and being within the very nature of man, the human, and ultimately being not only a signal of transcendence, but a sign of resurrection as well.

Humor is a virtue, but it is also a wisdom language as it speaks to us through the language of human life, observation, and experience. Humor is based on discrepancy, incongruity, absurdity, and unpredictability. In humor there is always a surprise ending. The joke always has a punchline and the ending is never what one expects. The discrepancy in humor can be between man and himself, man and another man or woman, man and animal, man and nature, with the ultimate discrepancy being between man and the universe. Being similar to resurrection, the ending will be a surprise. The discrepancy is what often causes something to be humorous. Good humor springs from the heart of man. Its essence is love, and it has the aromas of truthfulness, hope, honesty, and is grounded in prudence (wisdom) which is one of the Cardinal Virtues. Good humor never crosses the line into things like ridicule, sarcasm, scorn, mockery, buffoonery, and never deeply wounds another person through viciousness. Any humorous punchline depends on creativity, meaning, rhythm, and timing to create its desired effect.

Although humor can be considered a virtue, it is also a signal of transcendence and a sign of resurrection because the comic reflects the human spirit's experience of disjuncture from what ought to be universal and feelings of personal containment in a human body. The body housing the spirit is located presently in a seemingly absurd world filled with much anxiety, despair, disillusionment, and all of that simply ends in human death. This makes our spirit within us very uneasy in this world because at our very depths we know we are really at home elsewhere. The comic, in employing humor for its desired effect, seems to dance between two altogether different realms at the same time (similar to resurrection). Humor often arises from incongruity. The conventional thinking and logical reasoning is undermined by the seemingly absurd and divergent. There is often a juxtaposition of incompatible concepts and humor could even go as far as to employ outright universal absurdity such as the seemingly ridiculous idea that dead bodies could be rising to new life in eternity. Therein, once again, is the dance between the two altogether different realms.

Humor enables us not to take ourselves too seriously. By laughing at the discrepancy, irony, paradox, or incongruity we are doing much more than simply "whistling past the graveyard" (pun intended)." Humor allows us to realize that this discrepancy, implied disjuncture, and containment in an earthly body is not final and will ultimately be overcome. Humor points to that other realm where the dance is also taking place. The comic, in employing humor, transcends the reality of the human person's ordinary and everyday existence by positing temporarily a different reality in which the assumptive decisions and rules of ordinary life are suspended (once again like resurrection). Like humor, the dramatic tension between what is and what ought to be is both a personal and universal human experience. In fact, the word "humor" etymologically comes from a similar root as "human (man)," "humility" (not prideful), and "humus (dirt)." At each of their cores, neither humor nor resurrection takes death seriously.

Furthermore, it is the same well from which both comedy and tragedy have always drawn. This is the reason why we always see the two theater arts masks together, one laughing and the other sad. We never see them individually as together they express a contradiction and a paradox. The violation of our expectations is at the heart of the tragic as well as the comic. Man is the only animal that both laughs and weeps. This could be because man is the only animal that knows and can experience the difference between the way things are, and the way they ought to be. We can envision this extended to ultimately deny the gravity of life and death or even possibly to reflect our dying and rising as is the case with death and resurrection.[5]

The image of the embodiment of humor in the human person has historically always been the clown. The figure of the clown has the underlying intention of making people see themselves as embodied in the absurdity of the human condition. For a while, the clown can make the absurd seem even normal and can use humor to speak truth to the illusion of power. In ancient times the court jester assumed the role of the clown before the king. The clown has a way of suspending the ordinary and the usual by standing against, disrupting, or even reversing the normal order of things. Doesn't this all sound very similar to resurrection?

My favorite clown character has always been Don Quixote conceived by the first true novelist, Miguel Cervantes in the 17th century. Don Quixote was both an idealist and a clown as the defender of lost causes as he tries to right all wrongs. The story is part satire, part paradox, and a comedy and a tragedy rolled into one. The novel is simultaneously both humorous and spiritually profound. Even though Don Quixote, an elderly and humorous clown character, is powerless, he sets out idealistically tilting at windmills while wearing a wash basin on his head and riding on a sway-backed nag. In the end, the author Cervantes will show that even though reality changes Don Quixote, he will somehow change others' reality through his love, defense of lost causes, vivid imagination, and his idealism. It is his quest to follow that star, no matter how hopeless- no matter how far.

Finally, it is no accident that Cervantes has subtly positioned this lead character, Don Quixote, the humorous clown, to resemble Jesus Christ. The parallels are not exact and don't extend to every facet of the character, but there is little doubt that Don Quixote, after being subject to much ridicule and scorn, changed the reality of others. This includes Aldonza, who was transformed into becoming the beautiful Dulcinea. He accomplishes this through the purity of his love and his steadfast idealism as she slowly began to believe in what he saw in her. She ultimately came to believe in her own worth. Near the end of the novel, Don Quixote is lying on his death bed, moments from dying and in walks this beautiful, confident, elegant woman—She is angelic and truly a vision to behold. Don Quixote doesn't recognize her at first and asks her who she is. She replies, "My Lord, don't you remember? You sang a song, 'To dream the impossible dream . . . ' You gave me a new name when you called me Dulcinea. I am your lady, Dulcinea." Like humor (and resurrection), the story moves between two realms, the concrete world of stark reality, and the transcendent world of love's transformative power and unreasoned possibilities. It ends up being what literary critics throughout history have called not only a masterpiece, but truly "an impossible dream."[6]

There is not just considerable humor, but plenteous aromas of resurrection implied throughout this story. Although both humor and death are universal human experiences, are constants in history, and are a part of human life and experience; resurrection is not. We cannot say that like humor or death, resurrection is a thoroughly human experience. Because resurrection occurs on the other side of death, it occurs in another realm and therefore is similar to humor which due to its inherent discrepancy, irony, and contradiction, occurs in two altogether different realms. Furthermore, even though we might say that humor and resurrection are not exactly the same, they certainly do rhyme. This implies that we could envision humor not only as a signal of transcendence, but also as a sign of resurrection.

In closing, let me say that this book began by talking about H.O.P.E. as the Horizon Of Promised Expectation. In contrast, humor in many respects depends not on the expected, but on the unexpected occurring. The final "punchline" is always a surprise ending. That's what makes it humorous. Therefore, resurrection can be seen as an event which is less dependent on human hope as a Horizon Of Promised Expectation than it is dependent on human hopelessness. God will always be the God of the unexpected and the God of surprises. Because the resurrection of Jesus Christ as the first fruits occurred on the other side of human death, it transcends history. Because it is trans-historical, it will have its effect on the past, present, and the end of all history. Any hope for our own resurrection will be out of our power and control and always dependent on the intervening hand of the divine and the grace which is the gift of a loving God. Providentially, neither Jesus's resurrection nor ours will depend on human hope which would limit it to only our horizon of human potential and our vision of its reasoned possibilities. On the other hand, if we are listening with the ears of our heart, we might hear that divine echo of our self-communicating and loving God resounding within us.[7]

Finally, at Easter time in one of his homilies, my former pastor, the late Father Bill Shinnick, of St Maria Goretti Church in Lynnfield, MA, told a story.[8] He related how at a children's mass a few years prior, as the little ones were gathered and sitting all around the altar at Easter, Fr. Shinnick had asked the children a question. He asked them what they thought Jesus's first words might have been after his resurrection from the dead. Most all of the kids were stymied and had no idea what Jesus's first words might have been. After a time, one brave little boy raised his hand and as the pastor asked once more: "So, what do you think Jesus's first words might have been after his resurrection son?" The little boy stood up, threw his arms out wide, and then straight up in the air, and excitedly said: **"TA-DAH."**

NOTES

1. P. Berger, *Rumor of Angels*, Signals of Transcendence (Garden City, NJ, Doubleday & Co., 1969).

2. Ibid. Ch. 18 f. 1, pp. 61–90.

3. "Transcendental Anthropology," Karl Rahner, Ibid. Ch. 13 f. 2; see also chapter 13 of this book.

4. M. Hickey, *Get Goodness,* Virtue Is the Power to do Good (Lanham, MD, University Press, 2011, pp. 92–96).

5. "Humor" *Merriam Webster dictionary* online, https://www.merriam-webster.com /dictionary/humor see also *Encyclopedia Britannica* online https://www.britannica .com/topic/humor.

6. M. Cervantes, *Don Quixote*, Project Gutenberg, found online, https://www .gutenberg.org/files/996/996-h/996-h.htm.

7. Ibid. Ch. 1.

8. Rev. W. Shinnick, Easter homily, St. Maria Goretti Church, Lynnfield, Ma., April 15, 1979.

Index

About the Author

Michael Hickey is a graduate of Northeastern University, Boston, MA, and a Master of Divinity Studies' graduate of Weston Jesuit/the Boston College School of Theology and Ministry, Boston, MA. Following a career as a corporate executive for a Fortune 500 company, he became a director of two 501 C-3 charitable nonprofits.

He has had six books previously published: *Holy Silence, Themes from the Gospel of John, Get Goodness, Get Real, Get to the End,* and *Catholic Social Teaching and Distributism*. These books were published by University Press of America and Hamilton Books/Rowman & Littlefield Publishing Co., Lanham, MD.

Mr. Hickey is retired and spends spring and summer with his family in Dartmouth, MA, and fall and winter in Naples, FL. He teaches courses on religion and philosophy at Florida Gulf Coast University (FGCU), RA, Naples, FL.

His current work, *Rising Light*, is based on material he will be using in teaching a new course on Resurrection of the Body at FGCU.

Michael Hickey is married to Theresa, a published poet and an editor of all his books. In their fifty-eight years of marriage they have raised four happy and "well-adjusted" children into adulthood and they have seven beautiful grandchildren.